How to Understand Your Bible

Part 2

THE MYSTICAL CHRIST

HEAD OF CHRIST
BY TOUSSAINT DUBREUIL (1561-1602) ECOLE FRANCAISE

The Mystical Christ

RELIGION AS A PERSONAL SPIRITUAL EXPERIENCE

By Manly P. Hall

THE PHILOSOPHICAL RESEARCH SOCIETY, Inc.

3910 Los Feliz Blvd. — Los Angeles, Calif. 90027

ISBN NO. 0-89314-514-9
L.C. 52-18341

Copyright © *1951*
By the Philosophical Research Society
Eight Printing 1999

The Library of Congress Catalogued
The First Printing of This Title as Follows:

Hall, Manly Palmer, 1901-1990
    The Mystical Christ; religion as a personal spiritual
experience. 1ˢᵗ ed. Los Angeles, Philosophical Research Society, (1951)
            248p.   illus.   24cm.
        Part 2 of the Author's Trilogy:
How to understand your Bible. (New ed.)

            1. Mysticism   I. Title
BV5082.H34   149.3   52-18341
ISBN 0-89314-514-9

Published by

THE PHILOSOPHICAL RESEARCH SOCIETY

3910 Los Feliz Boulevard, Los Angeles, CA 90027
Phone (323) 663 2167 Fax (323) 663 9443
Website www.prs.org Email info@prs.org

Printed in the U.S.A.

TABLE OF CONTENTS

THE LABARUM OF CONSTANTINE

Chapter One

THE PATH OF FAITH

Mysticism is not a sect or a creed; it is a conviction, deriving its authority from the natural instincts of the human heart. The desire to know intensifies the rational faculties of the mind and the intuitive powers of the soul. The intellect approaches knowledge from the outside. It stands as an observer of the wonders of the universe, but it cannot experience what it discovers. The emotions do not exist or fulfill themselves on the impersonal level of rational procedure; they always desire to possess or to be possessed. It is the way of the heart to ensoul knowledge, to bring dead things to life, and to bestow its own warmth and light upon the aloofness of wisdom. Thus, as science seeks truth by impersonalizing that which is personal, religion achieves the satisfaction of itself by personalizing that which is impersonal.

To the mind, the story of religion is a historical account of man's spiritual, ethical, and moral descent. The spiritual experience of the race is of interest to the anthropologist, concern to the sociologist, and anxiety to the psychologist. Such worries and reservations are of no interest to the devout. The heart accepts only the essential fact of faith. It rejects neither the old nor the new, for its very reaction is timeless. The faith of the living is always the living faith. It is vital because it is immediately available. The instinct to believe is identical with the instinct to survive. To the skeptic, religion may be a constant cause of doubt, but to the believer, it is an ever-present help.

The soul of religion, like the soul of man, is locked within a material structure, and subject to those misfortunes and disasters which corrupt and destroy forms. When we meet another human being, we are not satisfied to know him only according to his outward appearance. We wish to understand him and to experience a degree of intimacy, by which there is a mutual sharing of things intangible and at the same time invaluable. We wish to know the person that lives in the body, and in like manner we desire to be known and not merely observed or examined.

The forms of religion are vast bodies ensouled by ideals and convictions. It is not enough to accept the forms or even examine the organisms and organizations which bear witness to the inner workings of doctrine. The desire to experience religion reveals itself as a quest for the object of a simple and natural devotion. We desire to believe, we desire to hope, and, most of all, we desire to be understood. We seek in our faith the satisfaction of instincts otherwise frustrated. We may be seeking security, but we can never be satisfied until we have discovered as a fact within ourselves the all-sufficiency of the divine power. It is from this urgent need for personal adjustment with faith that the mystical concept grew. By means of mysticism man bridged, by the simple act of faith, the interval between himself and God. While the mind defined the splendors and powers of Deity, the heart interpreted both the Divine Person and the divine purpose on the level of familiar acceptances. The venerating instinct accepted God through the experience of human parenthood, the benevolent instinct through the experience of human brotherhood, and the final relationship between Divinity and humanity through the experience of mortal love.

The mental faculties of the human being are ever alert to that kind of evidence, proof, or demonstration which will provide cherished beliefs with reasonable explanations. This procedure is long and difficult and usually leads to conflict and confusion. It requires a wonderfully ordered mind to achieve profundity without complexity. It is not unlikely that discussion will fall into argument, and that the ends which we seek will be obscured by the means which we use to attain them. The intellectualist is seldom comforted, inspired, or enriched as a person by his own thoughts. To him, thinking is a vocation or an avocation, and he can devote his entire life to technical processes and formulas which neither enrich nor improve his character.

The heart is not restricted or restrained by the intricate machinery of logic. It requires neither science nor philosophy to justify its convictions. Such support or defense as the mind contributes is acceptable, but not the determining factor. The mind is ever seeking satisfaction; the heart, security. Those who follow the dictates of reason desire to know and to conquer the unknown with the energy of thought. The emotional energies become impatient of this interminable curiosity. They demand no more of fact than is immediately available. It is not necessary to be a botanist in order to appreciate a flower. Its beauty may be the result of the workings of strange and mysterious laws, but the flower conveys a message by the simple fact of being.

As the botanist becomes ever more deeply absorbed in his studies of plant life, the direct impact of beauty is sacrificed. Research transforms the natural wonder into a scientific marvel. Eager to learn, he destroys the flower so that he can analyze its structure. In the end he has sacrificed beauty in his effort to understand the beautiful.

As knowledge feeds the mind, so beauty nourishes the heart. The intellect survives upon its uncertainties; the emotions, upon their acceptances. In a strange way thoughts are negative, and feelings, positive. The mind demands; the heart gives. Learning is a process of accumulation by which we seek to gather all kinds of information for the purpose of enriching the intellect. That which the mind so patiently collects becomes an ornament or adornment of faculties. The heart chooses rather to bestow or to give of itself. It responds instinctively to the invitation of beauty. It yearns ever to be one with the object of its devotion.

The religious mystery contains within itself all that is known and all that is unknown about life and living. The individual exists in an immensity of time and space, of consciousness and intellect, of energy and matter. All the diversified achievements of men are in substance spiritual, even though in appearance some of them may seem to be physical. The search for knowledge is motivated by the impulse to understand God and self.

Even while the mind is exploring the infinite manifestations of the divine power, the heart is striving to experience this power as an immediate fact.

Knowing with the mind depends upon the patient arrangement of fragments into patterns. Knowing with the heart is an immediate apperception of principles. We may ask if it is possible to possess truth without the laborious processes of analysis and estimation. Mysticism affirms that truth cannot be possessed even by the mind. By virtues peculiar to itself, however, the heart can be possessed by truth. We grow, not by demanding, but by accepting. This gradual transformation of attitudes is beautifully revealed in the Song of Songs, which is Solomon's. The king first sings: "My beloved is mine." Later he broadens his understanding, saying: "My beloved is mine, and I am my beloved's." Then, at the end of the Song, he speaks the heart doctrine: "I am my beloved's." The motion from the consciousness of possession to the realization of perfect renunciation is the path of mysticism.

The heart tells us that we gain all by giving all. In this way we know that through the love of God we experience the God of love. The heart actually becomes that which the mind is forever seeking. Even this miracle itself cannot be comprehended by the reasoning powers. They can accept it only as a miracle, and will reject it utterly if they have been schooled against the possibility of the miraculous. It is difficult to find a word which will describe the apperceptive faculties of the soul. Perhaps we can call them appreciative. Faith is first an appreciation of something which cannot be immediately known. We appreciate great music, beautiful works of art, and fine literature. This impulse of approval, together with acceptance, implies that we acknowledge superiority. If we appreciate that which is fine and have the instinctive ability to recognize true worth, we are said to have good taste. Refinement manifests as an instinctive recognition of values. Applied to religion, appreciation enlarges faith because it bestows sublimity upon God and his works.

Mysticism teaches the immanent availability of the divine power. It transforms, by a process of interpretation, all doctrines from codes into qualities of conviction. The religious story is accepted, not historically, but as an eternal fact of consciousness. Christian mysticism derives its authority from the teachings of Jesus and his disciples and especially from the writings of the Apostle Paul. It is probable that Paul himself had received instruction from the teachers of non-Christian sects. He studied the writings of the Jewish mystical philosopher Hillel, and was conversant with the doctrines of the Syrian Gnostics. There has been much controversy about Paul and his place in the descent of the Christian faith. He has always had a considerable following among Christian liberals, many of whom were sympathetic to the mystical interpretation of the Scriptures. Paul alone of those whose writings have been included in the New Testament preached "Christ in a mystery." Some accepted Jesus as the son of God, the promised Messiah, who was to redeem the faithful by his advent and ministry. Others were convinced that he was to become the redeemer of the Jewish nation and the restorer of its ruling house. Still others, rejecting the divinity of the man, saw in Jesus a noble and virtuous teacher who sacrificed his life in the service of humanity.

Paul, after his vision on the road to Tarsus, introduced a new dimension of understanding. He preached:

"Christ in you, the hope of glory." By this statement alone he revealed his deeper insight. It does not follow that all of Paul's opinions were equally lofty or applicable to future generations. Yet, throughout his writings are gentle and beautiful phrases and passages which reveal a sincere and searching heart. The preaching of Paul divided the Christian faith into two distinct concepts. One writer has referred to these as the Jesus of Peter and the Christ of Paul. The physical Church claims its descent from Peter, and has certainly emphasized the literal part of the Christian mystery. The mystical communion, which from its very nature could not be a vast organization, has descended from Paul and has bestowed upon the world those freethinkers and religious liberals who suffered as heretics from the persecutions of their more orthodox brethren.

Conformity with approved theological institutions does not satisfy all who seek religious inspiration. While many are content to follow in the creeds of their fathers, there are always a few who feel the need for a more personal spiritual experience. The rise of modern science has contributed to the rapid growth of mystical movements throughout the modern world. Many of the beliefs acceptable to our forebears are incompatible with present-day knowledge. In every instance the contradictions have arisen in the historical parts of the faith. It has become increasingly difficult to sustain the uniqueness of the Christian doctrine or to justify the exceptional place which it occupies in the religious world. Every part of the physical structure has been assailed or questioned. The authenticity of the Gospels themselves and even the historical existence of Jesus have been attacked. The nominal Christian, being in no position to debate the subjects in controversy, has been forced to accept or to reject without adequate evidence. Here the mind has taken over the guardianship of spiritual convictions, and the result has been a bitter controversy.

While the objects of his faith are being constantly undermined, the religious person still experiences within himself the need for faith. The disturbed state of present human society intensifies the longing for spiritual security. Many are beginning to realize that this security came not from their Church, but from within themselves. They bestowed their faith upon the creed or denomination which they accepted. Actually, the consolation which they imagined they had received from theology originated in a devout heart dedicated to truth. Christianity was not an institution but a conviction, guiding conduct and inspiring to the performance of good works. When a man became dissatisfied with the teachings of his sect, he sought a purer stream of instruction. After numerous adventures, a few came to the conclusion that religion was a private matter and not a public concern. When an intellectualist disagreed with his clergy, he became an agnostic; and when an idealist found himself in the same predicament, he became a mystic. The reasoning faculties addicted to the Aristotelian method were either in or out of the Church. The heart, rejecting such dramatic decision, resolved to keep the faith and to allow theologies to rise or fall with time.

After all, the Church was only the handmaiden of the doctrine. She preached what she believed, but it was the right of the human heart to weigh all things and cling unto the good. The corruptions of the Church had no effect upon the integrity of the spiritual content of religion. To reject the substance because a human organization was inadequate was foolishness. To so identify the substance and the shadow that both survived or fell together was stubbornness, not devotion. All bodies become infirm and ultimately perish. Truth itself cannot vanish in the dust, but is forever fashioning nobler forms through which to function. It may be that the modern materialistic beliefs that life has no existence apart from body, and that man has no immortal soul, have contributed to the notion that religion is identical with theological structures and cannot exist apart from them. The idealist will not accept such a doctrine. He prefers to hold as a sacred fact within himself that men can fail religion, but religion *per se* never fails men.

The mystic is not by nature combative, nor does he seek to discredit the works of his fellow men. He frees himself from entanglements which have become burdensome by the simple expedient of interpretation. He ensouls the literal with such overtones as are required to fulfill his own convictions. Thus he can attend the same church and listen to the same clergyman without discomfort. He perfects from within his own heart whatever may be deficient in the sermon. Seeking new meanings, he finds them by the very fact that he knows them to exist. Mysticism might have achieved a larger sphere of social influence had it been more militant, but a contrite heart is never militant, and fulfills its impulses in gentle ways.

Mysticism always increases when prevailing religious institutions are dogmatically narrow or reactionary. When too much emphasis is placed upon formal worship or the unquestioning acceptance of inflexible creeds, the natural instincts of the heart are frustrated and offended. No one can be happy if his faith offends his emotional instincts or outrages his mentality. No oppression can be more complete than a theological tyranny, especially if this reduces the spiritual mystery to the level of a physical despotism. The revulsion against mediocrity is really a defense of the integrity of principles. The mystic seeks in himself that which he has failed to find in his creed. The moment the search for reality is turned inward, away from forms and toward life itself, the deeper and more beautiful facts of religion become apparent.

It is usual to conclude that mystics are strange kinds of persons—religious misfits who have chosen to depart from conventional paths of devotion into a wilderness of intangible ideals. Nothing could be further from the truth. There have been moments in the lives of the more orthodox when they have temporarily become mystics because of emergencies. Whenever and wherever the immanence of God is urgently required, mysticism emerges as the most vital element in the compound of faith. Private prayer is a mystical ritual. It assumes that God is available to all who ask with real and simple sincerity. The moment an individual takes his religious conviction and applies it as a present source of strength or comfort, he accepts the omnipresence of the divine power. This experience of the acceptance of God and the powers of God is the basic mystical experience.

In the human life-way, faith usually emerges as reason fails. We put our trust in the sufficiency of material resources as long as these seem to sustain our requirements. Both the sick man and the physician have a common faith in medical knowledge until the disease is pronounced to be fatal. In that moment, skill relinquishes authority, and the future is returned to the keeping of the infinite power. In the presence of sov-

ereign uncertainty, we become aware of our place in an
infinite plan. It is now the plan which must carry on;
we can go no further. Resignation to the divine will
comes at the end of most lives, but at the beginning of
mysticism. Whether we know it or not, we live forever
in the substance of the divine nature. It was always
available by the simple act of acceptance.

It is a mistake to assume that the devotional attitude
is associated with limitation of intellectual powers. We
never actually outgrow the need for spiritual consolation. Primitive man was a mystic by instinct, and modern man becomes a mystic by intuition. The intellectual
faculties unfold from a state of ignorance to a state of
knowledge. The emotional nature unfolds from a condition of instinct to a condition of intuition. The security
of personal living is entrusted to the mind only in that
transition period between ignorance and wisdom. In
the closing years of his life, Plato passed through the
mystical experience. His magnificent mind made possible a more complete acceptance of the universal mystery. It was this transformation which so alarmed
Aristotle that he finally withdrew from the Academy
and formed his own school. Aristotle could not follow
his master along the narrow path that led from philosophy to faith.

The Neoplatonists of Alexandria were, for the most
part, men of outstanding scholarship, yet the concepts
which they unfolded were completely mystical. The
mind was disciplined to accept union with the divine
nature as the fulfillment of its own purpose. In the cycle
of life, the perfect faith of a small child is restored as
the perfect faith of the sages. We experience the divine
presence as we stand upon thresholds. It is present on
the threshold of material life, and it reappears on

the threshold which leads from this world to the one beyond.

As all religions include mystical content, so other departments of human activity have their spiritual overtones. We know that the theological instinct impels toward the conscious experience of God. The philosophical quest is motivated by the dynamic impulse to seek and discover truth. Even physical science is dominated by the irresistible urge to conquer the unknown and to approach the substance of reality. God, truth, and reality are merely three words with one ultimate meaning. They signify a state of union with the object of spiritual desire. It may well be that the mysticism which will be experienced through the extensions of scientific research will be the most dynamic spiritual impulse that has ever come to the human race.

St. Francis of Assisi found his union with God through humility, penance, and service. Baron Emanuel Swedenborg attained the same end from his profound studies in higher mathematics. The availability of the divine power through the natural and simple acceptance of the reality of that power is not restricted to a particular level of attainment. That which sustains and strengthens faith by revealing the certainty of God prepares the way for the experience of mystical identity. The child mind, by the circumstance of innocence, is without doubt or reservation. The mature mind, having transformed innocence into integrity through experience, justifies that which the child has accepted. It is during the adolescent period which lies between that the apperceptive powers are confused by those uncertainties which obscure essential values.

The term *faith* has been badly misunderstood. It is not the unquestioning acceptance of that which is not demonstrable, nor is it a blight upon natural curiosity. We are not less anxious to learn; in fact, thoughtfulness finds a fuller justification. Faith is the conscious and voluntary acceptance of the wisdom, love, and security behind and within the processes of creation. It is the recognition of a universal integrity so complete and so inevitable that human doubts are intuitively dissolved. Truth is good, law is love, and life is God. Once the human consciousness has accepted these facts, a sufficient faith is not only possible but also imminently available. Faith becomes a discipline of the heart, even as philosophy is a discipline of the mind. By the practice of faith, the emotions are refined and their excesses subdued.

When faith is strong in the heart, the mind is at peace and the body is without tension. Composure itself is essential to the integration of the human personality. The conflict which burdens those of little faith not only interferes with man's inner life, but also unsettles most of his objective activities. Where faith is weak, doubts are strong; and to doubt is to divide, to weaken, and to impoverish. We cannot be secure as individuals if we are without confidence in the security of the divine plan. If Nature be without purpose, then all human purposes are meaningless. Faith bestows courage because it substantiates the works of courage. It also justifies aspiration by supporting the human hope with the certainty of the divine purpose. It is the mystical conviction that God is present as a power within man. This power is remote and inaccessible as long as the human personality resists its works or denies its reality. Faith opens the heart to God by the discipline of quietism.

Those who seek truth are admonished to be still and know. In a wonderful way, faith bestows stillness. This mystery is the perfect work of faith. When we enter a vast cathedral and stand in the presence of sacredness, we are instinctively silent. We wish to accept the atmosphere of the holy place. The spell would be broken if we failed to be reverent. The sanctuary of God in man must likewise be approached with gentleness and peace. We worship most perfectly when we are quietly receptive to the impact of holiness. If, then, we seek the God who abides in the innermost, we must come with the simple dignity of sufficient faith. To fail in this is to profane the mystery of life and the source of that mystery. Faith, like love, cannot survive either analysis or definition. We may dissect the body of man, but we cannot in this way discover his spirit. Likewise, if we approach the mystery of God to weigh, analyze, consider, and debate, we find nothing. The divine substance cannot be discovered, it must be experienced, and when it is so known it can be neither named nor defined.

In Christian mysticism, Christ is the revelation of the love of God. It is difficut to decide whether love bestows faith or faith justifies love. Perhaps faith must come first. It is not easy to love that which we do not know or which is remote and majestic. If faith bestows the power to know God in the heart, it is inevitable that we shall love that which we have come to experience as beautiful and good. In the very process of worship, we instinctively bestow our love upon the object of our adoration. Faith, having known the fact of God, instinctively interprets that fact through the emotion of adoration. The word *adoration* means *divine love* or *affection on the level of the spiritual substance.*

The simple act of faith opens a new world and a new way of life to the human being. The physical universe is governed by laws that must be observed, and disobedience brings inevitable retribution. The spiritual state of man also has its rules and obligations, but few of us are aware of the strength of these gentler statutes. The Sermon on the Mount (Matt. 5:7) is the code of mystic Christianity. Many have said that these commendations cannot be applied in modern society. Minds and bodies may be governed by the Codes of Hammurabi and Justinian, but the heart alone understands and accepts the Beatitudes. The kingdom of faith is not of this world, but its domains are vast and its authority greater than we know. The path of faith is not one of sacrifice but of fulfillment. It is only when there is little faith that we must make those uncomfortable decisions between principles and practices.

Various impulses, not all of them meritorius, impel to the search for God. These impulses are as diverse and contrary as the convictions of the disciples about the ministry of Jesus. Some believe that spiritual achievement will bestow temporal authority; others, that it will compensate for weaknesses of character; and still others, that it will make available to them the material objects of their desires. While such ulterior motives are present, true faith is not possible. The heart which is established in righteousness seeks nothing for itself, requires nothing, and demands nothing. When we attain to a sufficient faith, all things that are needful are added. Miracles are wrought, not as the result of faith, but by the very fact of faith.

In *The Mystical Divinity* is revealed the doctrine of divine grace. The ever-available experience of the fact of God transforms the universe of law into a sphere of grace. There is no longer anything that is terrible,

ominous, or fearful. There is only divine love, working
in mysterious ways to perform its wonders. Man created
the god of wrath, which is a shadow without substance.
By the experience of faith, man comes to know the
God of love abiding in everlastingness. The mystical
experience is an act of becoming, which unfolds toward union with the sovereign good. There is no growth
or progress apart from becoming. We are not enriched
by what we have, but by what we are. Many have
turned from their religions because institutions have
not been able to bring peace or security to the world.
Theologians have forgotten that they serve best through
the unfoldment of their own spiritual powers and not
through the enlargement and glorification of their institutions. Religion has not failed, but the substitution
of formal worship in the place of the works of private
faith can never succeed.

Mysticism escapes from the illusion of history. It
frees the mind from its most natural inclination, which
is to approach events from the outside. The mind seeks
to possess facts by accumulating them and storing
them away for future reference. Having arranged them
chronologically in the filing system of memory, it considers itself to be well-informed. The heart has no time
for such classification. It bridges intervals of time and
quality by an instinctive appraisal of values. Mysticism
in this way accepts history only as a dated record
recording eternal verities. The records of nations are
long accounts of hates, fears, hopes, dreams, and intense
allegiances. While the manifestations of human instincts
may be divided and arranged chronologically, the instincts themselves are not susceptible to such organization. Scriptural writings are important because they
restate ever-present emergencies. The heart accepts

the lesson, but rejects the historical framework. It gathers all doctrines into an eternal now and experiences them as an immediate impact. In this way the old becomes immanent and can be experienced and thereby known in the spirit rather than in the letter.

This overcomes the prejudice against ancient writings and the insistent demand for new revelations. A revelation is itself only an interpretation of an enduring fact. Once the fact is known, the interpretations are no longer required. Mysticism is the direct attainment of the end rather than an intellectual reflection upon the means. We cannot plan growth as we would chart some physical project. Where Nature asserts her procedures, we have learned to accept them and to adjust to the situation which they cause. Spiritual unfoldment is also a growth according to the laws of the divine world. This enlargement of truth within ourselves is not the result of a demand or an insistence; it is the divine will accomplishing its own purposes. It would not occur to us that we would have the right or the power to dictate the growth of a flower or the physical development of another human being. We accept the unfoldment of these lives because we are ever in the presence of the process. The mysticism in our hearts increases in its own way. It is our privilege to accommodate ourselves to the spiritual plan of which we are a part. Once faith has revealed the reality of our divine nature, we are inspired to serve the requirements of this nature. Like good gardners, we can protect the soul-flower, but we can never dictate its unfoldment.

The German mystic, Jakob Boehme, wrote that the seed of Christ had been placed in every human heart. It was the privilege of man to guard this seed and to nourish it so that it could grow. The food of the soul is love, faith, and beauty, and when this nutrition is properly provided the soul enlarges and extends itself until it becomes a great tree and bears its fruit, and this fruit is for the healing of the nations. Like a palm tree growing in some desert place, it gives shade and rest and even food to the lonely traveler. It is the tree of Christ growing from the human heart that brings peace to the world and contentment to the individual. The gentle, thoughtful, and devout meditation upon this wonderful and beautiful symbol enriches consciousness and causes the mood of mysticism. The mystic walks in ways of beauty because he believes in the ministry of beauty. He knows within himself that beauty bears witness to the divine love and the divine wisdom. He needs no further evidence than that which is available to all through the simple instinct of appreciation.

Christian mysticism was certainly inspired by the sect of the Essenes, a small community of devout men and women which flourished in Palestine in the opening centuries of the Christian Era. The Essenes venerated truth by the simple act of living according to its laws. They dwelt together in socialized communities, sharing their goods in common, and devoting their lives to the service of all in need. They recognized no formal worship except personal prayer and collective industry. The Essenes proved in their day, and other mystics have demonstrated the same fact in later generations, that the love of God does not interfere with social usefulness. The mystic is not one forever absorbed in the contemplation of eternal verities. His inner experience impels him inevitably to the practice of the ideals which possess him. That which he experiences in private he applies publicly. He may be misunderstood and even persecuted, but if he is truly strengthened by God his faith sustains him. It is the intellect which is content to live in a world of thoughts. The heart cannot be so constrained, but escapes through good works into a larger sphere of usefulness.

The 13th chapter of I. Corinthians is one of the most beautiful parts of the New Testament and powerfully substantiates the mystical content in the Christian communion. Paul the apostle addresses the Church of God at Corinth, exhorting the congregation to be united in faith, saying to them: "Know ye not that ye are the Temple of God, and that the Spirit of God dwelleth in you?" Paul then devoted much consideration to the mystery of charity. Before we consider his text, we must free our minds from the peculiar limitations which the word now implies. The Greek original is *agape*. Our English word *charity* is from the Latin *caritas*, meaning *dearness* or *love*, from *carus*: *dear, costly* or *loved*. At the time of the translation authorized by King James, and even earlier, *charity* literally meant the virtue or act of loving God with a devotion transcending affection for creatures, and of loving our fellow men likewise for the sake of God. It also implied the substance of love unfolded to its perfection and, hence, Divine Nature itself, or God.

Charity in the sense of generosity to the poor or the afflicted or the support of benevolent institutions or public provision for the underprivileged is to be understood only as an expression of, or an action impelled by, the internal experience of the mystery of love. Paul, therefore, was not primarily preaching charity as good will to the poor, but as the love of God manifesting through the natural inclination to serve those who are in need. In mysticism, we must further examine the substance of love and discover within it the secret of all worship and the perfect law of all human relationship. The life-way of the mystic-Christian is inspired and directed by a quality of personal realization by which the understanding is strengthened in the resolution to practice the presence of divine love in daily works. The meaning of Paul is clearer to us if we use the word that now most clearly states the essence of charity. He writes: "Though I speak with the tongues of men and of angels, and have not love, I am become as sounding brass, or a tinkling cymbal . . . And though I have the gift of prophecy, and understand all mystery, and have all knowledge; and though I have all faith, so that I could remove mountains, and have not love, I am nothing . . . And though I bestow all my goods to feed the poor, and though I give my body to be burned, and have not love, it profiteth me nothing . . . Love suffereth long, and is kind; love envieth not; love vaunteth not itself, is not puffed up, doth not behave itself unseemly, seeketh not her own, is not easily provoked, thinketh no evil; . . . beareth all things, believeth all things, hopeth all things, endureth all things . . ."

Paul clarified the meaning of charity in his own words, for he reminded the Corinthians that bestowing all earthly goods to feed the poor was not a proof of love, but profited nothing without the spirit of love. All Christian mystics have been noteworthy for the humility and gentleness of their lives. In most instances, this was not an attitude cultivated in the hope of attaining grace; it was the simple act of devotion resulting from the internal acceptance through faith of a conviction about truth. If humility is assumed, if patience is cultivated to impress others, there is no support from within the self. Under such conditions, the practice of these artificial virtues ends in suffering, frustration, and disillusionment. There is no reward from the world, or at least there is no certainty of such reward, for the practice of these mystical virtues. The source of security is completely internal, and survives because it bestows all and requires nothing - not even appreciation.

It requires clearer vision than is available to those who "see through a glass darkly" to know that to give all is finally to possess all. Today each is seeking security, peace, happiness, and health. To attain these most desirable ends, numerous means have been devised. Most of these have failed because they have been motivated by selfishness. The dimensions of the failure are apparent, but the lesson has not been learned. There is still an abiding hope that we can build a better world by protecting ourselves and preserving our own opinions. The mystic will sometime be recognized as the most practical of mortals because he has renounced the policy of private gain at public expense. He is further relieved of pressure because the spiritual alchemy taking place within his own consciousness has transmuted material ambitions into spiritual aspirations. Ambition impels one to dominate and to possess on the material plane. Aspiration inspires one toward a sharing in truth by the act of becoming like truth.

The peoples of Eastern countries have long appreciated the powers of the soul. They have created systems of soul-culture like those which the Greeks called disciplines. The first of these disciplines was intended to strengthen and enlighten the human standard of values. It has been said that where man's treasure is, there also will be his heart. When we really desire the gifts of the spirit as we now crave the satisfactions of the flesh, we will naturally and simply sacrifice the lesser for the greater. Mysticism has been called a path of pain, not because its way is one of suffering, but because most are brought to a recognition of realities by temporal or physical misfortunes. We seek only that which we need, and we seldom realize our internal needs until our external estate is threatened.

In the human experience, suffering nearly always resolves itself into a question. We wonder why our policies have failed and how we can remedy the condition. Thus uncertainty inspires a larger effort to discover the rules governing human activity. Insecurity impelled the developments in religion, philosophy, and science. We have discovered much and become apperceptively aware of still more. Yet, with all our seeking, we have not achieved either peace or security. The quest must continue, and the examples of those most wonderfully enlightened remind us that only the mystical experience can make available the spiritual resources of mankind. We can conquer the furthermost and remain creatures alone and afraid, but when we allow our hearts and minds to be conquered by the innermost, the long journey comes to its end.

Each human being is distinctly and inevitably a person. By this virtue each has his own dreams and aspirations and a group of faculties and powers within his own composition suitable to advance his cause. Mysticism does not require that we depart from the familiar or attempt a way of life that is strange or distant. We do not grow by assuming a code that is contrary to our inclinations; rather we unfold by and through that which is familiar. The mystical experience is not associated with any one profession, art, or craft. There is no such royal road to God. All constructive human purposes have their mystical overtones, and as we approach the perfection of our own work, whatever it may be, we become aware of its spiritual content. All labor, whether it be of the mind, the heart, or the hand, shares in the quality of service. Motive becomes the magical agent. The refinement of our own motives leads inevitably to the realization of the eternal mystery. When the motive is profit, we labor in darkness, but when the motive is the simple love of God and man, we work in the light and toward the light. It is then, and then only, that work satisfies the soul. Mysticism is not the end of labor, but the beginning of truly meaningful and satisfying endeavor.

The mystic does not renounce knowledge; he does not deny the wonderful accomplishments in all fields of learning. To him, all these achievements become better roads and paths. Because his understanding is deeper, his appreciation is more enlightened. Thus we say that mysticism is not a science or an art, but an ensoulment of sciences and art. It ends by a conscious consecration of all things known and all things knowable to the service of the Great Cause, which is the source of the known and the unknown. Do not, therefore, in the search for truth depart from your own world with its joys and sorrows. As you grow, that which is not your own will depart from you. Neglect no responsibility, reject no work that comes to your hand, but fulfill all things, and all that is needed will be fulfilled in you.

Mysticism is wonderfully suited to the problems of each generation. No matter how simple or how complex living may be, the power of the heart is always available and sufficient. Times may change, states may rise and fall, religions may be reformed or neglected, prosperity or adversity may dominate society, but faith is unchangeable. It accepts equally the appearances of good and bad, and cannot be corrupted by external emergencies. Love, hope, and faith are eternal and are part of that timelessness which pervades all time by a spiritual dimension. It is for this reason that mysticism has flourished among the members of every belief that has come to the world. The interpretations of religion are many and diversified, but the mysticism is always the same. It is the heart fulfilling its own requirements, nourished and sustained by the presence of God.

During the last several years there has been a rapid increase of popular interest in retreat movements. Many denominations, which have not hitherto encouraged retreats, have established houses devoted to religious seclusion. Persons from many walks of life have testified to the benefits derived from brief periods of voluntary retirement from the pressures of society. This in itself reveals the urgent need for mystical content in the compound of the human personality. It explains the existence of monastic Orders and why they have survived the innumerable changes which have affected the outer form of society. To the mystic, religious houses are symbolical of that internal existence available to those who withdraw from a state of objectivity. Even as the external is perpetually agitated, the interior part of life is nearer to that tranquillity which is the condition of God.

As the small child, frightened or injured, instinctively hastens to its parents for protection and comfort, the mature person in a state of emergency seeks the consolation of his faith. God becomes the understanding father-mother, which we try to find by the simple processes of visualization and acceptance. The Divine Presence is available by the act of voluntary acknowledgement. We believe, and by the direct action of belief we perform a personal retreat toward participation in the condition of godliness. The Christian mystic accepts as a fact that by entering into his own quietude he will come into the substance of the Divine Presence. This is the act of faith, and the burden which has impelled the action is unfolded through the mystery of prayer. This is the meaning of the words of Jesus when he admonished his followers to enter into the dark closet and pray to their Father in secret.

The mystical mood is one of prayerfulness rather than a formal ritual of prayer. It is not conceivable to the human heart that the Eternal Parent must be addressed as though it were a person apart. Faith itself accepts the omniscience of God and approaches with the full expectation of being understood. In mysticism, to seek is to find, and to knock is to have the door opened. All that is required is internal certainty about the reality of things unseen. When faith is deep and sufficient and love is pure and unselfish, all things are possible. So strengthened by simple convictions, the mystic experiences within himself the Sacrament of the Eucharist. He is the living chalice, and in his own heart the water of penance is miraculously transformed into the wine of ecstasy.

It is evident that mysticism leads to the most intimate spiritual experience possible to the human being. The practice of the Presence is fulfilled in the fact of the Presence. As long as religions are the instruments of the heart doctrine, they will be custodians of the mystical tradition. When we wish to share that which is most real or most sacred with another person, we have a *heart-to-heart* talk with him. The very term implies that we choose a meeting place remote from superficial or artificial concerns. In the practice of our religion, especially under great stress, we seek a rela-

tionship with God which is heart-to-heart. Our need is
not satisfied by the God of battles or the Lord of hosts,
nor do we find contentment in the splendor and majesty
or power of the divine nature. We long for the simple
assurance of God's love, which, even more than God's
wisdom, surpasses understanding.

The life and teachings of Jesus of Nazareth as recorded in the Gospels has appealed for centuries to
those of devout heart. The simplicity of the basic story,
the strangely quiet and gentle atmosphere which pervades the account, and the humble background of the
disciples and followers of the Nazarene have combined
to convey a wonderful impression of spiritual integrity.
The first Christian communities survived by faith alone,
and there is no intimation that philosophical interpretations were involved or that the need of them was
felt. It was only after the Church attained a large
sphere of temporal authority that scholarship was introduced. Even during the scholastic period, intellectuals were more a cause of concern than of satisfaction.
As Christianity spread into classes accustomed to a more
philosophical type of spiritual nutrition, the mystical
overtones were compromised. In the effort to justify
and to prove on planes of logic and reason, the simple
dignity of honest convictions gave place to argument
and debate. Faith, diluted by doubt, no longer guided
the religious impulse. While men cast lots for the rai-
ment, the garment itself was destroyed.

In a strange way Christian philosophy destroyed
Christian mysticism, and in so doing impoverished the
world. Philosophy leads inevitably to interpretation,
explanation, or the substitution of ideas. Sectarianism,
which is, indeed, a thorn in the flesh, is justified and
sustained only by interpretation. It is the conviction of

the mystic that the life and teachings of Jesus should not be explained; they must be accepted as an experience of consciousness. The moment we examine and analyze the fabric of love, it vanishes, and the same is true of faith. The simple impact of a holy example and the direct appeal of a kindly and gentle teaching penetrate to depths not to be reached by proof or evidence. The interreligious effect of Christianity clearly reveals this fact. The informed members of all non-Christian religious systems have frequently expressed, both as individuals and through their leaders, their profound respect and admiration for the life and teachings of Jesus. Many have accepted him on the level of their own saints and inspired leaders. It is the mass of Christian theology accumulated through the uncertain means of interpretation and explanation which has offended, or at least disturbed, the devout non-Christian and Christian alike.

If men are to meet in fellowship and dedicate their common efforts in good works, it will not be because of the industry of conflicting creeds. As surely as the mind divides, so surely the heart unites. Only in the mystical experience of faith can we accomplish the dynamic fact of spiritual co-operation. We must learn, and by now all necessary evidence is available. The human heart is the common denominator of all convictions held devoutly to be true. All mystics practice one quality of faith regardless of the names or terms by which it is described. This quality of faith is the hope of the world. Most persons must achieve this quality in the silence of their own hearts, but once they have known it they are united as one person in the love of God and dedicated as one person in the service of good.

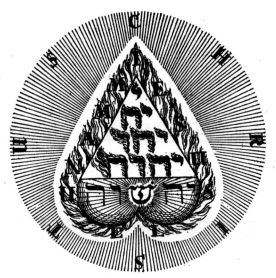

JAKOB BOEHME'S SYMBOL OF ILLUMINATION

Chapter Two

THE SOCIAL MYSTICISM OF THE ESSENES

Two thousand years ago the Roman Empire ruled the world. Its military arm conquered vast areas, and its political ambitions were advanced in defiance to those natural laws which pertain to human rights. Desolated communities and devastated regions bore silent witness to the tyranny of might. The horrors of war were followed by the sorrows of slavery and the inevitable disintegration of cultural institutions. The victims of Roman aggression were sickened by their losses, and the victors, if we may believe the more intelligent Romans, were sickened by their gains. The waters of the Mediterranean washed the shores of a sad, tired, and broken earth. It was inevitable that out of this great pain in the hearts of the poor and the bereaved there should be born a mystery of faith. The sorrow of the world gave birth to the Man of Sorrow.

30

From the fall of the Judean Monarchy, which may be dated from the destruction of Jerusalem, 586 B. C., the Jewish people became increasingly more dependent upon their spiritual heritage. They matured philosophically and deepened the foundations of their cultural institutions. This unfoldment brought with it an appreciation of Greek learning. Alexander the Great made a friendly visit to Jerusalem, and whether or not the account given by Josephus is completely factual it reveals the over-all picture. The sympathetic meeting of hearts and minds, though made possible by Alexander's courteous presence, was substantiated by the spirit of Aristotle, whose wisdom had enriched the character of the young Macedonian. It is of historical importance that the three great conquerors who influenced the destiny of the Jews in ancient and modern times—Alexander, Caesar, and Napoleon—always treated these people with kindness and justice. Ambitious underlings were responsible for the tragedies which have so disfigured the political and social history of Jewry.

After Pompey captured Jerusalem in 65 B. C., the Jewish people found themselves unwillingly and unhappily involved in Roman politics. An example of their predicament was the occasion when Caligula proclaimed his own divinity and required public worship. The Jews were the only subjects of Rome who flatly refused to acknowledge the emperor's godhood. Caligula's assassination in A. D. 41 terminated the difficulty as far as Rome was concerned, but in distant Judea the incident had created bitterness between factions, accompanied by outbreaks of violence and the creating of lasting animosities. The cold detachment of historical perspective can in no way convey the personal sorrows and misfortunes that must be borne by those who live in troublous times. We can estimate pain only in terms of our own pain, and by the same means we can come to an appreciation of those forgotten heroes who resolved to keep faith with their God at all costs.

The mystic always derives his strength from deep and hidden places within himself. Thus internally sustained, he continues in ways which his heart dictates. Because he is moved by his heart and not by his mind, he is not inclined to an aggressive or belligerent statement or practice of his ideals. This gentleness and natural humility have protected most mystical communities. The members of these groups have been respected for their sincerity and good works even by those of other faiths. This was certainly true of the Essenes, who were permitted to live and worship in their own way during those periods otherwise difficult and dangerous. Most men, though themselves corrupt, honor the simple quality of goodness, and even the Roman was first a human being and then a citizen of Rome.

There were many mystical sects in Syria and the Lebanon. They differed in some particulars, but their prevailing attitudes and customs were similar to those of the Essenes. In the barren hills near the Dead Sea, the Essenes had established their community at a place called Engedi. The Order was not numerically impressive, and at no time did the membership exceed four thousand. Their sphere of influence was due solely to the simple virtues which they practiced. The Essenes must be numbered among God's meek who shall inherit the earth. They were a plain people, gathered from many levels of society. A man was not born an Essene; he became one by the spiritual hunger in his own heart. The heavy-laden came among them and found rest.

It is a mistake to assume that the Essenes were simply agriculturists and craftsmen. Some had been scholars or wealthy merchants or successful tradesmen. Each in his own way had found it impossible to continue practices which offended his soul. He had, therefore, divided his goods, bestowed his properties, terminated his wordly career, and returned to the natural faith of his fathers. Simplicity is most attractive to those who have long struggled with the complications of human nature. The mystical communities were not opposed to the world, which they deemed a good and proper place; they were opposed to worldliness, a strange, insidious, corrupting influence which attacked hearts and minds and destroyed the natural dignity of the human estate.

The mystic, having experienced the fact of the Fatherhood of God and the brotherhood of man, celebrated the former in his meditations and reveries, and practiced the latter through founding and maintaining a socialized community. All artificial divisions of race and class were ignored. It was accepted without question that all men were created free and entitled to equal opportunities. The Essenian settlement was a miniature democracy, a modest communal entity—an island of peace in a sea of chaos. It succeeded on a small scale because each of the members knew why he had chosen to be there and required very little leadership or guidance. There was no idleness among the Essenes, but there was protection for the young and repose for the aged. The group was not endowed nor was it financed by the State; it was supported entirely by its own members, whose gain from lawful enterprise was kept in the common purse.

The term *lawful enterprise* was interpreted as honest and honorable work. No activity was considered superior to another. Each of those who came bestowed his talents and abilities, but practiced them only according to the convictions of conscience. There was a broad rule against merchandising. The Essene could not buy the goods of one man and sell them to another; he must create or produce, and not barter or exchange. He was not supposed to hold public office, because by so doing he would be forced on many occasions to violate the dictates of his own heart. He refused to take part in war because he held life to be sacred. The Romans respected the Essenian code, and exempted all members of the community who were in good standing from military service. As many who sought refuge in the settlement had no inclination to continue their previous occupations, they had no special skill suitable to their new way of living. These farmed the surrounding land and performed such labor as might be required for the common good. Some apprenticed themselves to craftsmen and learned new trades.

The life of the Essene was divided between labor and learning. That the intellectual level of the community was high can be gathered from the historical accounts of the sect. Essenes were selected as teachers of the young, and Roman officials residing in Palestine selected these mystics, preferring them to scholars of other Jewish sects or tutors sent from Rome. Under the gentle guidance of these godly men, children received not only learning, but also enlightenment. The emphasis was upon the unfoldment of character and the cultivation of moral and ethical graces. The Essenes were occasionally called upon in matters of State, but always as impersonal counselors. They would speak only the truth and were incorruptible. Efforts to bribe them or intimidate them were entirely useless.

Some of the Essenes practiced medicine and healed the sick without charge. They were especially mindful of the poor, who could not afford to engage physicians. When the Essenian doctor attended a patient, he would not only prescribe a remedy, but would also clean the house, do the mending and washing and any other task which sickness had interrupted. If some gift was forced upon him by one of the grateful, it was placed in the general storehouse of the sect. Possibly influenced by older Syrian traditions, the Essenian community favored carpentry and building. It seemed to them that the building of a house was an appropriate symbol of building human character and a better world. To work with the hand was especially commendable, and the skilled craftsman, bringing comfort and security to homemakers, was contributing to the well-being of society.

There is a report that the Essenes traced the origin of their community to the visit of Pythagoras, who had traveled through the Near East on his way to Asia. We have no proof that the sect was devoted to higher mathematics or the deeper abstractions of philosophy, but in some respects they showed Grecian influence. Their religious principles were essentially devotional, and they required no more theological scholarship than was available to the humblest of their group. They could only meet in perfect spiritual equality by interpreting holiness as the unselfish service of God through helping his children. The Essenes held children in special regard. The Order adopted orphans and reared them with all tenderness. They trained these young people and were attentive to natural abilities and inclinations.

When these children reached maturity, they were in no way required to accept the teachings of the sect or to become members. They might choose to do so or not, as they pleased. The Order required or expected no compensation for service of this kind, for the good deed fully rewards itself.

The community could be selected as a collective guardian for the young or the old. Sometimes one of the more prominent Essenes was made the administrator or executor of an estate. Goods entrusted to him were protected by his life and honor, and if he asked to be removed from this trust it was a public indication that the estate was being mismanaged by members of the family or others beyond control. The Essenes also permitted their community to be a place of temporary refuge or retreat. Anyone could come among them as long as he respected their ways. The stranger might ask counsel, discuss his problems, and unburden his heart. All confessions were confidential. Simple and kindly advice was given, but no effort was made to convert the visitor to the doctrines of the sect. Incidentally, this was probably the most powerful method of converting. Those who left never forgot the gentle brotherhood, and many returned years later to this place of peace.

Among the Essenes, there were some who had received the gift of prophecy and could interpret dreams and visions. Such powers are often associated with advanced mystics. Josephus, the Jewish historian, mentioned a certain Essene named Simon who interpreted correctly the strange dream of the ethnarch, Archelaus. Although some mystical practices of this sect were regarded as heretical by the orthodox Jews, the Essenes were accepted as a curious but kindly group, whose ways were beyond the comprehension of average persons. There was no crime among them, they kept no slaves, and they acknowledged no masters. The group was also remarkable for longevity. So simple was their way of life and so moderate their habits that many of them attained to one hundred years of age.

It was general knowledge that the Essenes practiced mystical rites and kept sacraments peculiarly their own. They taught the corruptibility of the body and the immortality of the soul. It is believed that they accepted the doctrine of metempsychosis, but this is not known with certainty. The immortal part of man was held within the body as though imprisoned. Through disciplining the flesh, releasing the mind and heart from all worldliness, and dedicating the life to good works, the soul could be liberated and could finally ascend to the subtle, airy region from which it had come. More specifically, the release of man's higher self was not a departure from the corporeal part, but was a refining and purifying of the body, thus permitting the light within to flow forth into more perfect expression. In this way the body became the servant of the spirit and not its master.

The Essenes taught that good souls, when they had become perfect in righteousness, came in the end to a happy, peaceful, and radiant habitation in a beautiful land beyond an ocean. This region was the one which they had experienced in their hearts and for which they yearned with natural piety. Josephus points out that in those abstract parts of their doctrine, the Essenes held convictions similar to those of the initiated Greeks. Whatever their secret rites may have been, the public rituals of the Essenian sect were practiced through honest toil. They taught that the sweat of honorable labor was the true water of baptism.

Like the Pythagoreans, the Essenes held communal prayers before sunrise. There were also private prayers and times set apart for secret worship. They said grace before their meals, and the words were those of gratitude and thankfulness. Because of their way of life, they asked nothing of the divine favor except the privilege of serving in its name. They refused no request for help, even though it was unreasonable, and were without pride. The members did not own even the simple robes which they wore. Each kept his own garment clean and mended, and when it was no longer serviceable received another from the communal storehouse. The members were distinguished for their cleanliness and tidiness at a time when these were not prevailing virtues.

There were two distinct groups within the Essenian Order. The higher group was dedicated to absolute continence and rejected marriage and all human ties and relationships except spiritual fellowship. Men and women were equally eligible to both grades of the Order. The lower group was composed of householders who could marry and raise families and keep their simple homes in the community. Those living in wedlock were avowed to purity, and marriage among them was looked upon as a mystical sacrament. All members of the brotherhood refrained from adornment, wore no jewelry, and renounced vanity. Members of the lower grade who were childless took into their houses the children of relatives, and provided by adoption the homes for orphans.

The aged were held in the highest esteem, and it was remembered that they had worked faithfully and lovingly as long as their strength had permitted. Those who were sick or injured were given constant and devoted care and protected from all want to the end of their lives. The Essenes accepted the processes of life as proper and decreed by God, and in no way resented the infirmities of years. By virtue of this attitude there was very little sickness among them. Furthermore, they believed that growth toward God was a joyous experience. There was no place in their faith for despondency. By perfect acceptance they attained peace and serenity.

The celibate group was perpetuated either from the lower grade or by new members who had been drawn to the Order by the spiritual consolation which it offered. Through the circumstances of time, some of the members of the lower grade were left alone. These naturally drifted further into their mystical preoccupations. In these ways the sect perpetuated itself for several centuries.

Mystical communities are closely associated with the social currents of their times. The Essenes met a peculiar need, and, having fulfilled this requirement, they faded slowly from the memory of history. Even while they flourished, only three writers — Pliny, Josephus, and Philo — gave them particular notice. There is no record of the decline of the Order. They came, they labored, and the rest is silence. Some believe that Essenianism was absorbed in the larger stream of Christian mysticism. Like John the Baptizer, they preached in the wilderness, and when the Messiah came their work was done. Almost nothing is known of the Essenian sect after the end of the 1st century A.D. They were a link between pagan and Christian mysticism, and were absorbed into the new faith or into the orthodox Jewish communities as the result of the conflict between the Christians and the orthodox Jews.

Modern religious writers, in an effort to explain the beginnings of Christianity, have considered the possibility that Jesus was an Essene. There is considerable circumstantial evidence to sustain such an assumption. The humble manner of the man Jesus and the quiet patience with which he unfolded his ministry, together with the social implications scattered throughout his teachings, are essentially Essenian. On the other hand, there is no direct reference to the sect in the New Testament. This in itself is strange when we realize how closely the doctrines parallel. It is possible, of course, that old records were defaced or mutilated by those zealots who were resolved to protect the uniqueness of the Christian dispensation. It is a further wonder that non-Christian historians and philosophers of the period never raised the question.

Social mysticism has contributed a tremendous impulse to the advancement of civilization. The great religious teachers of the past were inspired sociologists, and the codes which they gave to the world always emphasized the application of spiritual convictions to personal and collective conduct. The virtuous man must not only be true to his God, but must also keep faith with his fellow man. Civilization is, therefore, the record of religion in action. It was impossible to believe in the wisdom, love, and justice of God without being moved to act in accordance with the divine will. Even under an autocratic system, the governor was inspired to benevolence, and the people to integrity.

The mystical vision extended horizons and intensified resolutions. It was the will of God that his creatures should dwell together in peace, security, and contentment. No explanation of this fact was necessary, for it could be experienced as a certainty of consciousness.

Men are not easily moved by forces operating outside themselves, but they cannot resist internal compulsions. Civilization is a motion from within man. He releases his social instinct in the same way that he draws a picture, writes a book, or composes a piece of music. By strengthening the idealistic and benevolent instincts of the heart, mysticism first civilizes the person, and through the person transforms the physical environment.

The Essenian community revealed the Essenian conviction, and in so doing exposed the natural mystical concept of a social order. Many times in subsequent history, mysticism again revealed itself and always the content was the same. The more confused and corrupt man's political and economic institutions became, the more clearly the human heart restated its determination. Consciousness does not seem to evolve; rather it emerges. In those periods when its outflowing was the most abundant, we had eras of enlightenment. Conversely, when this spiritual current ebbed, there were long centuries of benightedness. Men do not dictate progress; they become instruments of a motion greater than themselves. We grow by the increase of light, and not by the multiplication of laws.

Our faith in modern democracy is strengthened by the sincere belief that it is a way of life coming from the heart. If we are correct in this assumption and remain true to our faith, we can, and will, protect the rights of man as a statement of worship. In this regard, we require of the mind that it shall build enduring foundations of wisdom and skill to support our dreams. In The Gospel According to St. John, 13:34, 35, Jesus makes a statement of profound social import: "A new commandment I give unto you, That ye love one another;

as I have loved you, that ye also love one another. By this shall all men know that ye are my disciples, if ye have love one to another."

The application of this commandment in the political, economic, and social spheres would result in collective peace, security, and contentment. To the mystic enlightened love is the universal medicine. It is the only permanent remedy for those evils which have their origin in hate, selfishness, and pride. The human heart accepts as an experienced fact the reality of the gentle teachings of practical co-operation. Yet, so knowing and so believing, we permit our institutions to expand without adequate ethical overtones. This inconsistency is responsible for those individual and collective dilemmas in which we find ourselves. Society must be preserved because of man and not in spite of man. Mind has enriched us by strengthening the faculty of individuality, but this enrichment in no way relieves us of ethical obligations. We now have the conscious privilege of voluntary co-operation.

A gracious and loving action need not be justified or explained. Long before the technique of psychology was systematized, it was common knowledge that destructive thinking corrupted both the mind and the body. Must we reduce the fact to a formula before it is acceptable? Are we more inclined to guard our thoughts because we are convinced that the law of cause and effect operates on the plane of mind as surely as in the material sphere? Experience shows us that psychologists themselves continue to contribute their full share to the negative thinking of mankind even though they are fully aware of the processes involved and the consequences to be expected. The results of ethical or religious indoctrination must be carefully

examined if the real values are to be discovered. Those
who live well within some framework of spiritual or
philosophical doctrine are generally persons who would
have lived equally well in almost any situation. They
brought their own integrity with them and simply unfolded it through some accepted pattern. Thus we find
many beautiful and devout souls in all faiths even
though the sect itself may not be setting a very good
example.

Even congregational worship lacks significance except to those who inwardly experience more than is conferred by rituals. Faith remains, as it has always been,
an intimate association between the individual and his
consciousness of God. Public worship without private
conviction is only a formality. Thus, in substance, man's
relationship with the spiritual source of himself is
always mystical. A religion means to him exactly what
it brings out of himself by a process of interpretation.
It is easier to respond to impulse than to injunction. We
may not understand or appreciate what others recommend, but we do accept without question that which
we instinctively know to be true. Inward spiritual guidance reveals itself in ways adjusted to our daily needs.
It comes to us in terms which we can appreciate, and
inspires us to some immediate course of action.

Where mysticism motivates conduct, it flows
through ourselves into collective society. We live outwardly, but from within ourselves. It becomes our moral
duty to bear witness through conduct to the majesty of
conviction. To fail in this is to break faith with something we know to be beautiful and necessary. Yet, as
we look about us, we may be disheartened by the lack of
spiritual content in the civilization which we have
fashioned. We wonder how a creature with so many

advantages can so consistently corrupt his own institutions. Certainly Nature did not teach him to abuse and misuse his opportunities. Nor does God require disobedience to his own laws in order that his creatures shall advance their cultures.

The most obvious explanation is a gradual process of man obscuring his own values and coming, in the end, to dwell in a world fashioned in the likeness of his own confusion. Social systems rise and fall without a conscious realization of the universal plan. By focusing attention completely upon the objective productions of the mind, we have disordered our sense of values. We look about us for inspiration when we should look within us for guidance. We are surrounded by a sphere of unorganized and disorganized intensities. If we pattern our own conduct from the conduct of others, we must share in their disasters. We cannot commit the same offense so often or so devoutly that it can become a virtue. Facts remain even though no one believes in them, and error is no less unfortunate because it has an impressive following.

Mysticism teaches those who have shared in its vision that in solving collective problems the way *in* is the way out. The mystic is not selfish when he seeks the restatement of his own essential values. It is the motive rather than the action which determines the degree of merit. It is the right of each citizen to withhold his co-operation in situations which outrage his sense of integrity. It is also necessary that some in each generation preserve the eternal faith. It is only after we have solved certain problems in our own natures that we are able to make a significant contribution to society. Jesus told his disciples to seek first the kingdom of heaven and its righteousness. We have no way

of finding the world of spirit except by retiring into
those internal depths which bring us close to the eternal
power. Once we have experienced the consciousness of
God, we can appreciate the destiny of civilization. Until
then, we are part of a motion which is incomprehensible.

Although each generation is burdened with peculiar
abuses and some levels of human society are always
corrupt, essential progress from the heart continues and
is manifest in many ways. We have overcome, or more
correctly outgrown, many of the abuses which burdened
the past. Slavery is almost completely abolished. The
conditions of the young and the aged have been vastly
improved. We are also increasingly aware of world
needs and are generous in our efforts to relieve priva-
tion and suffering. The dignity of the human estate is
protected by unfolding legal codes, and the life expectancy has been lengthened through hygiene and sanita-
tion. Opportunities for self-improvement are increasingly abundant and religious tolerance is more widely
practiced than heretofore. All this and much more reveal a real and natural growth and the progressive enrichment of human consciousness. We have not failed;
rather we have not yet completely succeeded. There is
more to be done, and the work must be inspired by the
simple impulse of brotherly love.

Social mysticism may in some instances attempt
more than ordinary experience can sustain. The idealist
lives in the future, in a better world which is the product
of nobler instincts. Because of this visionary tendency,
the mystic is called impractical. Reactionaries insist that
we cannot fashion a world according to the heart's desire, but must forever compromise with contemporary
pressures. Light cannot temporize with darkness, and

truth reduced to the level of error loses all of its strength. The laws of the wise are not designed to regulate the conduct of the foolish, but this does not mean that wisdom from the heart will not ultimately rule the world. There can be no experience of fraternity apart from a sincere aspiration to world peace. We desire that suffering shall end and that all men shall dwell together with kindness and charity. Even as we live we see encouraging evidence that trial and error are strengthening man's resolution to perfect his institutions.

In order to achieve, we must have a purpose to which we can dedicate our lives and our honor. The architect first designs his building and then assembles the elements and materials necessary to its completion. To the mystic, God is the Great Architect—the Master over all those craftsmen whose combined labors must enrich and beautify the creation. Each man is a master builder serving the Supreme Artificer. Just as it took centuries to complete the massive cathedrals of Europe, so it may require thousands of years, or even longer, to perfect the Everlasting House. It is the privilege of each of us to true a stone and to place it properly in some part of the edifice. If our stone is securely set, others can put theirs upon it, and so the building grows. But if each stonecutter trims the rock only according to his own taste or the mood then upon him, there is no certainty that it can be used without further loss of time and effort. For this reason, the master of the workmen who gathered to build the temple of Solomon the King went each day at noon into the *sanctum sanctorum* and there received the work of that day traced by the living finger of the Supreme Architect.

The social commonwealth must be unfolded according to a proper trestle board. The plan is complete only

in the heart and mind of God. To know the work of the
day, which for man is supreme knowledge, each must
go to the sanctuary and receive his allotment of labor.
To the mystic this means a prayerful and humble receptivity. He kneels before the flaming altar of his own
heart and asks for his portion of labor. The voice of the
innermost speaks through the oracle of the heart, and a
little part of the plan is thus revealed. The workman
knows that he builds not in vain, and he asks no more
of comfort or consolation than this certainty that he is
keeping faith with the past and preparing the way for
the future. In this manner we have the great democracy
of works under the absolute autocracy of the divine will.
Those also serve who are hewers of wood and carriers
of water. No part is more or less when all are necessary.
When the Great Architect calls us to labor, we bring
the skill or the strength that is ours. There is always a
place which needs our offering. When, at the end of day,
the Master of the work calls us to rest and refreshment,
we are content, for we know that we have served.

In this way mysticism frees our hearts from the limitations of selfish and impermanent enterprises. We no
longer think only of ourselves, nor do we see the works
of our lives crumble about us, nor again must we leave
our dreams to a future that will not understand. There
can be no remorse for those who fulfill the instructions
of the Great Architect. The foundation of the house is
upon a solid rock of truth and not upon the shifting
sands of popular conceits. There can be no fear where
faith is strong, no despair when hope is incorruptible.
To build with life for life is to share in a certain victory.
We build not for now but for the ages, and the ages shall
bear witness.

Men are most grievously afflicted with uncertainties when their hands and minds are idle and their hearts are without devotion. Much of the restlessness, confusion, and discord that we see about us exists because men have not found their Great Work. Daily labor merely to provide creature comforts is not enough to satisfy the wonderful consciousness within us. Our many faculties, powers, and abilities demand full use and expression. The mystic is happier and more peaceful than those not so internally enlightened because he has found his work. He knows what must be accomplished, and he is ready to contribute everything that he is and everything that he has to the task.

Contentment is not, therefore, rest from labor, but a call to larger effort. Some may interpret the mystic life-way as an evasion of common responsibilities. This is a false judgment, however, on insufficient evidence. Man can never be happy unless he is creating, and most of all he yearns to create a better world. Even if he does not believe that he shall live to see the completion of his hopes, love strengthens him. He builds for love of those who shall come after him; he wants his children and their children to have a security which he has never known except in his heart. The individual is ever ready to sacrifice himself to causes which are worthy of this sacrifice. He dies on the field of battle to protect his country and his home. He gives his life slowly and painfully on the economic battlefield to supply the needs of those he loves. Why, then, should we doubt that, enriched by deeper vision, these same fathers and mothers, husbands and wives, brothers and sisters, who have given of themselves so generously to protect their little worlds, would not also in fuller and larger measure find fulfillment in the service of an eternal plan?

Experience also has shown that sincerity of purpose can be advanced by simple faith as surely as by substantial knowledge. If the heart tells us that we should perform a certain task, we are not inclined to debate the issue or to question the authority of the impluse. The idea that we must understand all in order to do anything is an intellectual approach to a mystery, the substance of which is beyond the reach of the mental faculties. Complete understanding comes at the end and not at the beginning. We grow in order that we may understand. The mind can help us to avoid unreasonable attitudes and practices, but it cannot bestow a quality of spiritual participation which must be earned by simple and sincere devotion.

It is everywhere evident in the unfoldment of the universal plan that man has not been equipped to proceed from certainties; rather he must advance toward them, sustained first by a quality of dedication. Because he advances toward knowing and not from knowing, he must grope his way out of the darkness of ignorance through the twilight of uncertain certainties to emerge finally into the light of truth. As this is the appointed way, the mystic accepts without complaint that which he cannot comprehend, convinced that by this obedience he fulfills the wonderful purposes of God. Thus, instead of seeking to understand the mind of heaven, he asks only to so live and conduct his affairs that he will be worthy to receive into himself the impressions of the heavenly mind and to serve these impressions with faith and a good hope.

The experience of living finally impels the individual to the recognition of universal principles. These are sensed or realized as remote in substance, but imminent in manifestation. The acceptance of the fact of universal consciousness, within which the Planner, the planned and the planned-for exist together, bestows a sense of internal security. In the light of this conviction, circumstances order themselves, everything becomes meaningful, unreasonable doubts and fears are dissolved, and we know ourselves to live and move and have our being within the benign sovereignty of the divine consciousness. Such a realization, if it is honorably attained, must constructively influence conduct. We inevitably adjust our habits and practices to meet the dictates of our concepts. If this does not occur, then our beliefs are intellectual acceptances and not convictions of consciousness.

It is the province of knowledge that it shall bestow skill. We learn in order that we may apply learning to our numerous activities. If study, then, increases proficiency, it fulfills itself through action. In like manner, faith confers a kind of skill to the works of the heart. It strengthens resolution, intensifies values, and dedicates conduct. From such an enlargement of internal values, we may naturally expect a more enlightened and benevolent quality of personal conduct. The individual himself should be strengthened and comforted and should manifest these attainments as love, patience, and composure. In Nature, all causes must produce their effects, and where the effect is absent there must be a deficiency of cause. We cannot love God with a true devotion and remain unreconciled with his creatures and his creation. We cannot understand the mysterious fact of truth and at the same time doubt the works which it causes and sustains. To accept God is to accept life also and to live in a continuous state of acceptance. It is understanding and not criticism which solves difficulties and dissolves uncertainties.

The Essenes resolved to live by the laws of God in a world of men. We have no evidence that flowers know why they grow or what their destiny will be. They fulfill themselves, each according to its own kind. By simply permitting consciousness to guide conscience, and conscience to govern conduct, the Essenes unfolded the basic plan for human society. The more devoutly they practiced these principles, the more obvious it became that the program was both possible and practical. Practice led to the personal experience of Truth. By loving their fellow men and serving them, the Essenes discovered in their own hearts the God of love and service. Other sects held the same beliefs, but many were content with a mental acceptance. As a consequence their doctrines remained sterile. Following along the way that faith impelled, the Essenes found themselves experiencing the natural fact of social democracy. With them it was neither a political ideal nor an ethical formula; it was the inevitable communal relationship of honest human beings. Democracy happened to them because they were guided by the love in their own hearts.

Aggressive types of reformers are inclined to criticize mysticism and its exponents. The man of action is more impressed by the quantity of activity than the quality thereof. He considers the quiet acceptance of the divine plan to be negative and nonproductive. Perhaps there are also two sides to this problem. Does the obscure mystic practice his principles in vain because he lives and labors and dies unknown, unhonored, and unsung? Is he defeated by circumstances because his contemporaries are unaware of his existence or decline to be affected by his endeavors? We are admonished by our Scriptures to sow the seeds of our good works, but not to be mindful of the harvest. The universe has spiritual dimensions which we do not fully understand, and that which appears to be the least among men may be the greatest in the presence of God.

The mystic is certain in his own heart that those who labor in the cause of truth do not labor in vain. They are contributing to collective human consciousness on a plane of subtle and invisible influences. If the light shining in the devout heart sends but a feeble ray into the world of forms, it may at the same time emit beams of extraordinary brilliance in the more subtle atmosphere of soul power. In this way, that which cannot reach humanity from the outside because of material density can nourish and strengthen our fellow creatures from within themselves. We are nourished not only by bread, but also by the energies of the soul. The mystic devoutly believes that the love in his heart enriches the lives of all created things. Love and faith and hope do not perish because the loving, the faithful, and the hopeful are apparently defeated in their efforts to enlighten others. All good thoughts and good deeds flow into a qualitative reservoir where they are available to each aspiring mortal in his hour of need. Where we add to the substance of collective integrity, we are making a greater contribution to the spiritual security of the race than when we strive so valiantly to correct a particular defect in human society. The good man may be obscure in this world, but the quality of his convictions is not obscure in the universe of values.

The wisdom and love of the ages are as surely accumulative as ignorance and hate seem to be. If we each inherit our part of an ancient disaster, we share also in the heritage of hope. We are spiritually stronger because we share in all the good that has gone before. The nobler parts of our civilization have come to us through the patient sacrifices of noble men and women whose names are not even remembered. Their efforts mingled together have become a mighty stream of soul power. Those who have served God in secret have been made manifest through the consequences of their devotion. The Power which marks each sparrow's fall is not indifferent to those who serve and wait and watch. We are better because of the good that has gone before, and the future will be still better because of the good which we add to the present store.

The realization that the practice of the divine presence is itself a great and wonderful service to others comes as a natural result of mystical devotion. If we believe that collective prayer has power, can we deny that collective conduct on the plane of prayer is even more powerful? Is not unselfish service in the spirit of God a constant prayer uttered into action? Words without works are dead. Which, then, is the true worshiper: one who preaches or one who practices? In times of national emergency, our churches unite their congregations, beseeching divine intercession. Is not the mystic fully justifed in his belief that to the degree that he keeps the faith, the faith will keep him?

It is most unlikely that the Essenian community expected to be remembered in the descent of world idealism. The Essenes left no writings, inspired no particular reforms, and taught no formal doctrines. They quietly walked in the light and had fellowship one with the other. These devout people probably were a little saddened when their minds informed them that their tangible accomplishments were slight and transitory. They had achieved little, but they had attained much. Far away in China, the wonderful old teacher Confucius died of a broken heart because the world had re-

jected a teaching which he knew was desperately
needed. Later China deified the kindly man whose last
words were: "I have failed." It is not wise, therefore,
to estimate with the shortness of human vision the consequences of right effort. The servants of truth are under the protection of heaven and are content to accept
its perfect works.

Life is either a state of rebellion or a state of acceptance. It seems that both courses are necessary, but
experience shows that all rebellion must end in acceptance. We have no authority of ourselves, for it is
the Father in us who doeth the works. We are fulfilled
to the degree that we fulfill the Father. The mystic, from
his own internal experience, knows that he is useful
no matter how small may be his sphere of influence.
If he is faithful in little things, he will earn the right to
a larger opportunity. This comes not because he seeks
it, but as an inevitable consequence. He accepts the
larger task with the same humility and the same dedication. He is moved into his proper place, not by his own
will or his own ambition, but by the power of God.
Where faith is real there can be no impatience, for in
the heart there is no essential difference between the
large and the small.

The rise of Christian mysticism was only the perpetuation of the heart doctrine. It was expressed through
new symbols and associated with new names, but its
substance was unchanged. It is not important to establish the historical descent from one sect to another;
rather we should be interested in the perpetuation of a
substantial spiritual fact. To the mystic, all things are
mystical. As the Christian faith expanded, the life of
Jesus of Nazareth was accepted mystically as an experience of consciousness---a mystery in the spirit.

BYZANTINE HEAD OF CHRIST
FROM A SEPULCHER

Chapter Three

JESUS, THE SON OF MAN

Countless books have been written about the life of Jesus and the significance of his ministry. As we survey this mass of literature, it becomes evident that Jesus was the most controversial personality in the history of our race. Although most of the writings are reverent and respectful, there are some calculated to disillusion or prejudice the mind, and a few dedicated to the proposition that Jesus never existed and that the whole story of his life is a pious fabrication. Each author proves his case to his own satisfaction, but not always to the satisfaction of his readers. The difficulties are due primarily to the lack of historical records. The accounts contained in the Gospels still remain the only source of biographical material, and fragments gathered elsewhere are without general acceptance.

The four Gospels contain conflicting statements which are not easy to reconcile. These inconsistencies encourage criticism which more solid scholarship, for lack of evidence, is unable to meet. Even the most orthodox readers are perplexed when they attempt to synthesize the available reports. It seems almost incredible that a man like Jesus, with such dynamic spiritual and social convictions and able to perform miraculous acts, should have left so slight an impression on the pages of history. Nor was this due to the lack of historians, for lesser events of the same period have been fully recorded. It is only fair to say that the origin of Christianity is obscure and that modern research methods and facilities have been almost completely ineffective.

Most of the biographers of Jesus have justified their efforts by recourse to interpretation. They have attempted to apply the words of the Master to the several departments of human effort and enterprise. One sees Jesus as the physician; another, as the jurist; still another, as the economist. These points of view are often interesting, sometimes valuable, but the books cannot be considered biographical in the strict sense of the word. The human effort to interpret obscure portions of the Scripture or to fill in the frequent lacunae has led to sectarianism rather than illumination. The various translators of the New Testament have added to the general confusion by the firmness of their opinions and the weakness of their insight. They have added so much of interpretation to their translations that the reader is deprived of an impartial text.

We point out these difficulties in order that we shall not be accused of being uninformed. We feel, however, that enlargement upon controversy will serve no useful purpose. It has not done so in the past, and there is no reason to assume that it will do so in the future. The subject can only be historically clarified by the discovery of new and authentic records. Until such time, the Christian faith must stand upon the foundation of the four Gospels and the spiritual, ethical, and moral instructions which they contain. The entire subject is shifted by force of circumstances from the historical to the ethical level. We will advance to the common destiny more rapidly by examining the contents of the message and by allowing the historical issue to rest in peace.

Among the most controversial of the words of Jesus are those which refer to his relationship with God. Are these to be accepted literally or are they to be interpreted according to a mystical sense? Without a fuller understanding of idiom, it is hard to know the original implications. The orthodox-minded have accepted without question the words themselves, yet there is no religion or philosophy in the world which has been adequately taught on the level of terminology. Jewish scholars have never refused to accept the reality of a mystical tradition concealed within the formal structure of their Scriptures. They believed that the soul of the law (the Mishnah) was concealed within the body of the law (the Torah), even as the soul of man is hidden within his corporeal nature. Even deeper and more remote is the spirit of the law by which all things are justified. This explains the Scriptural statement: "The letter of the law killeth, but the spirit of the law giveth life."

Mysticism always seeks to escape from the limitations imposed by literal utterance. Even our most carefully selected words fail to convey the fullness of our

intentions unless there is understanding in the heart of
the listener. Even as the mind receives the wording,
the heart seeks the overtone, searching for the soul of
the idea which is locked within the letters and syllables.

It is not certain from the Gospels that the disciples
themselves, or whoever recorded the events, were aware
of these overtones. Each interpreted both the man and
the ministry in the terms of his own insight. Later
religious writers, now regarded as venerable, sought
according to their own needs and recorded according
to their own convictions. The result has been an accumulation of tradition sanctified by human authority,
but not necessarily a true revelation of original meaning.
Here, again, the modern devotee is victimized by pressures which he has neither the learning nor the inclination to resist. He assumes that the long acceptance
proves much, when in reality it proves only the long
acceptance. Even the Bible student, completely dedicated to an earnest desire, may be seeking in this
world for a religious substance which is not of this
world. If so, he searches in vain and shares in the error
of the disciple who believed that Jesus was sent from
God to restore the physical monarchy of Judea. One
literalism is in quality no different from another.

That the mistake has lingered and enlarged and
become glorified there can be no doubt. The very
physical structure of Christianity, with its magnificent
churches and cathedrals, its rich and powerful clergy,
and its perpetual bid for temporal authority, has no
justification in the teachings of Jesus. The very attempt
to build a Christian Empire in the mundane sphere
requires a generous interpretation of the words of the
Master when he stated definitely and firmly that his
kingdom was not of this world. If we feel ourselves

equipped to amend this simple and apparently incontrovertible revelation, why do we debate fine points of meaning? A religion cannot survive the vicissitudes of time without interpretation. Principles must always be stated in terms of the familiar and applied to particular events and conditions for which no provision had originally been made. In practice, this interpreting procedure nearly always involves some degree of compromise. We hope to gain a little by sacrificing much.

Mysticism is not nourished by the clash of creeds. The mystic has passed through the experience of sectarianism without finding solace in the confusion. He neither criticizes nor condemns those who are working out their salvation according to the dictates of individual or collective conscience, but seeks a more intimate experience of the Christian mystery. His heart tells him that he must live the life if he is to know the doctrine. Argument is most general among those of little faith. To conform or to accept with the mind requires slight effort and brings only slight reward. The secrets of the heavenly kingdom are reserved for those who keep the laws of that kingdom. From the beginning of the Christian dispensation, there have been a few who accepted the life of Jesus as a magnificent example of spiritual conduct. It might be more honest to say that these mystics have experienced their own concept of the life of Jesus and have found it completely soul-satisfying. It never occured to them to ask whether Jesus lived or not; they knew that he exemplified a way of life which led to spiritual integrity and personal security.

Mystics have referred to Jesus as "the way" and "the gate." The quality of personal integrity which he personified or embodied is its own authority. The ac-

count is spiritually true even though it may be historically unprovable. Fortunately we are preserved by our
convictions and not redeemed by our historical acceptances. The good man is the fact even though his career
is never chronicled. Those not mystically inclined find
it difficult to understand the power of faith and its effect upon human character, but, if they are so minded,
they can glean from history the useful information that
faith is the source of progress, and fear is the source of
corruption. Using the mystical key, therefore, we approach the life of Jesus, not simply because we admire
a good man, but because his way of life bears witness
to the eternal life-way which all the world is seeking.

The comparative approach to religion and folklore
reveals the universal distribution of the concept of the
world hero. Every important cultural system has resulted in the creation of an embodiment---a person,
historical or mythological---through whom the heroic
attributes of the collective consciousness are revealed.
In all cases, the folk hero is the heroic self, and the life-
adventure of the hero is a kind of parable telling one
story in the terms of another. We are accustomed to so
interpret the wanderings of Ulysses and the exploits of
Siegfried. We associate these embodiments directly
with certain dominant cultural impulses. Regardless of
the original intention, the account of the life of Jesus
has taken on this complexion. He is not only the spiritual
ideal of countless millions, but also personifies a level
or quality of moral and social conduct. He is the example of that which is devoutly believed and certainly
held to be true.

The mystic instinctively recognizes that two mysteries are mingled together in the Christian story. Perhaps this was once more evident than it is now. The

processes of interpretation have confused the patterns, but internally we have certain faculties of discrimination which refuse to accept the confusion. Our spiritual need requires the twofold realization, and this need cannot be denied. There is Jesus, the son of man, and Christ, the son of God. We accept the fact that Jesus was Christened, but not that Jesus was the Christ. As the folk hero, Jesus is humanity, considered individually or collectively. Christ is the redemptive power of God, the Supreme Being manifesting through and upon the human creation. Christ is the son of heaven, and Jesus the son of the earth.

The mystic ascends through the experience of Jesus by consecration and purification. The noble example of the Nazarene becomes the life-way of his followers. If they would know his mystery, they must obey his instructions: "If ye would be my disciples, take up your cross and follow me." The story of Jesus as given in the Gospels is, therefore, the eternal account of the truth seeker. Each in his own way and according to the convictions of his own conscience must walk in the footsteps of the Master. It is only by so doing that he can experience the mystical redemption. The basic conviction is fashioned from older spiritual traditions. When the Jews were wandering in the wilderness, they carried with them a portable sanctuary which was called the Tabernacle in the wilderness. This was a walled enclosure surrounding a wonderfully ornamented tent divided into two apartments. The multitudes worshiped outside the walled enclosure, bringing their offerings to an altar adorned with the horns of rams. Those of greater sanctity were permitted to enter the courtyard where stood the laver of purification, ornamented with the mirrors of the women of Israel and supported on the backs of twelve oxen. Only the priests could enter the holy place within the Tabernacle itself, and the high-priest alone was permitted to stand in the holy of holies and behold the glory of the Lord hovering between the wings of the cherubim.

The human being seeking to experience the mystery of God must walk in the way appointed. Whosoever shall attempt to enter by another way, the same is a thief and a robber. Approaching the entrance of the universal sanctuary, the wanderer comes first to the altar of burnt offering. Here he must offer up to God not only the first fruits of his labor, but also those attributes of personality which conflict with honest aspirations. It is good to give of what we have, but in the mystery of the spirit it is better to give of what we are. Later, the truth seeker comes to the laver of purification. This is the first baptism, which is of water that washes away sin. We interpret baptism without the thoughtfulness of the heart. It really means purification from worldliness and dedication to the works of truth.

The life of Jesus, like the Mystery rituals of the ancient temples, describes "the perilous journey." Jesus personifies the eternal neophyte seeking admission at the gates of the spiritual universe. This may be accepted intellectually with slight profit. It is not the acknowledgment but the experience that works the miracle. As the Chinese Taoist visualizes the Transcendent Being within himself and then strives to strengthen that being by consecration to its substance and service to its will, so the Christian mystic meditates upon Jesus as a mystical personification of his own higher nature. In this sense, Jesus was immaculately conceived. He was born of the virgin—the power of the soul—and he came as the fulfillment of the divine promise. Though des-

tined to be ruler over kings, his birth was humble and he
lay in a manger surrounded by cattle. He was born
while Mary and Joseph were on a journey, as required
by the edict of Caesar.

In the very process of paying tribute to the powers
of material sovereignty, man experiences a spiritual unfoldment. It is in the very despotism of the physical circumstances of living and the tribute that we must pay
to the institutions we have created that the needs of our
souls are most clearly revealed. Although Jesus was
said to have been born miraculously, the genealogies
were compiled to show that he was descended from the
royal line of David and was the rightful king of the
Jews. Thus he emerged in the dual role of the priest-
king, ruling by authority of heaven and the traditions
of men. He was described later as a priest forever after
the Order of Melchizedek, priest-king of Salem. There
is no profit to be gained by attempting to reconcile the
immaculate conception with the genealogies. The mystic understands what is meant, and the meaning is true
and clear.

Shepherds first saw the star of Jesus, but we have
failed to grasp the meaning of the symbolism. In the
bleak, dreary land of Palestine, flocks of sheep were not
grazing in the cold dead of winter. The term *shepherd*
was used in many faiths to signify the religiously enlightened or the leaders of spiritual groups, and the
crosier, or shepherd's crook, was the insignia for their
office. These were the ones who saw the star which
shone over Bethlehem, and they paid homage to the
wonderful teacher who had come to labor, to suffer,
and to die among them.

The beams of the star were also visible to three wise
men of the East, who came to bring their offerings of

gold, frankincense, and myrrh. They traveled far to visit the babe in the manger, and because of the wickedness of Herod they returned to their own homes by a different road. Many interpretations of this symbolism suggest themselves to the receptive consciousness of the devout. Perhaps the most intimate and therefore the most universally applicable is to liken these Eastern sages to the enlightened mind, the illuminated heart, and the dedicated hand. All three give of skill, knowledge, and understanding, and they offer themselves and their kingdoms to the service of the consecrated self. If other interpreters say that the wise men revealed through their gifts that they represented the three parts of the moral universe, which we call heaven, earth, and hell, the significance is the same. If a scientist prefers the terms life, intelligence, and force, these are still the gifts which wisdom makes available to the service of the God in man.

Herod, who personifies worldliness and all those false concepts which depend upon ignorance for survival, was duly alarmed by the advent of spiritual resolution. He had been warned of great changes to come by John the Baptizer, who cried out: "Prepare ye the way of the Lord, make his paths straight." Is not this John forever preaching the new dispensation? Reformers, educators, and idealists have not only pointed the way of essential progress, but they have also proclaimed the inevitable victory of right over might. According to the Bible story, Jesus, while yet a babe, was taken away into Egypt to escape the slaughter of the innocents. Here, again, we have an intimate mystical circumstance. Herod, of course, represents the prince of this world, who has nothing in truth. In the instant of personal dedication to principle, conflict arises within us. We want to enjoy the benefits of enlightenment without sacrificing the egoism which is at the root of our disaster.

The flight into Egypt is another example of the old symbolism. The ancient name for Egypt meant *darkness* or *obscurity*. To escape the persecutions of worldliness, the human spiritual conviction retires and takes refuge in the quietude and obscurity of the inner life until it is strong enough to proclaim its ministry. Before the Egyptian Temple of Harpocrates was the figure of the child-god with one finger upon its lips admonishing silence. Mysticism has always been the silent way. It reveals itself, not in words, but in gentle deeds. It is better that conviction be made known by a light shining from the heart, which can be perceived by those who possess inward vision. Egypt was the old way of learning, and there the new way found haven against its enemies.

John the Baptizer was also an embodiment of the wisdom tradition. He personified both the ancient teacher and the ancient teaching. As the voice of the old, he announced the new, and we find him proclaiming the mystical fact that the crier in the wilderness shall decrease, but the light of the world shall increase. This is the way of faith and of all simple and natural seeking after truth. Learning points the way and even announces the advent, but it is the spirit in the heart that is preferred. Through Salome, John was sacrificed to the injured pride of Herodias, but not until he had baptized Jesus in the waters of the Jordan. The old sanctified the new and received the evidence of the divine mission. This was the man of flesh who gave way to the man of soul.

Little is recorded of the childhood of Jesus. In some of the apocryphal writings, it is said that he helped

Joseph in his carpenter shop and was a gentle and duti-
ful lad. If the account given in the Talmud refers to
Jesus of Nazareth, he may have made a second journey
to Egypt to study there and to be accepted into the
sacred rites. The report that Jesus traveled to the Far
East has not yet been substantiated by reliable historical
data. These occurrences may be true, but they are not
essential to the unfoldment of the principal theme. The
man of soul grows within the living environment of the
unfolding human personality. He brings his own light
from the aeons of light and is not dependent upon formal instruction. At this stage of the mystery he bears
witness to the will of heaven and not to the wisdom
of the world.

In the proper season, Jesus entered the synagogue
and there discoursed with the Elders. He confounded
them with his insight and left them disturbed because
they could not understand. These Elders were the faculties of the mind that had explored the Torah and even
the Mishnah, but had not experienced the spiritual substance of the law. They were amazed at the gifted child,
but were not prepared to accept him as soul power.

We must also understand the environment in which
the eternal drama was unfolded. Herod Antipas, as te-
trarch of Galilee, was actually a vassal of Rome. It was
usual for the Romans to permit the States that they
governed to administer their own internal affairs, especially in religious matters. Beyond the power of Herod
and his successors was the authority of Rome in the
person of Caesar. Even though there may be historical
inaccuracies in the Bible account, again the essential
pattern is appropriate. Caesar personifies the collective
form of human society. He stands for government from
the outside manifesting through the machinery of man-

made law and human authority. Within this collective scheme, each person has a certain measure of freedom. He governs himself, but is subject to the pressures of world policy. The complex of faculties, powers, and energies which impel the individual who has not as yet attained spiritual selfhood is revealed as Herod, who had autonomy within his own domain, but had to be obedient to Rome. Caesar, like modern society, permitted each man to practice his own faith as long as it did not conflict with the privileges of others. This is a wonderful key to mystical convictions. Man is not prevented by material law from unfolding his spiritual graces. There is always internal freedom once man has released himself from slavery to his own ambitions.

To the degree that we sacrifice the most sacred and honorable of our convictions for the advancement of our temporal estate, the man of soul is condemned by the man of body. It is meaningless to hold antipathy against classes, races, or religions and accuse them of betraying the principle of good. Each man betrays himself, and it is for this reason that the laws of Nature require that each man also redeem himself.

After the baptism, Jesus gathered his disciples, taught his doctrine, and performed his miracles. If this ministry be understood as an internal growth, it is no longer remarkable that history preserves only the consequences, for these alone are manifest. The selection of the twelve disciples was an extension of the earlier symbolism of the twelve tribes of Israel. This is further shown through the second circle of seventy-two disciples corresponding with the six elders who were chosen from each of the tribes. The number twelve symbolizes wholeness or completeness. The Pythagorean dodecahedron, a twelve-faced symmetrical solid, implied the universe. The man of soul draws the twelve powers which constitute the sum of the human potential. He gathers them about him as the instruments of his work. He therefore calls them from their several humble labors, and they follow him. This calling of the disciples is experienced as a natural part of mystical unfoldment. The light of the soul touches all the resources of the personality and they open to him like flowers opening to the light of the sun. These powers, or disciples, were one with the light before the beginning of the world. They labored in darkness until they answered the call of the carpenter.

The ministry was unfolded in the circle of the sanctified. They formed the ecclesia, or the living church. This was the church of the Holy Grail described in the mystical romances of the Age of Chivalry. Before the completion of the ministry, the Master empowered the twelve to perform in his name the works of salvation, but among them was one who had not the wisdom and betrayed his Lord. It was in his place that the apostle Paul was established. Jesus also instructed the multitudes in parables. Here the multitudes represent those factors of environment not actually within our own natures. These must be taught by the perfect parable, which is the mystical way of life. They must see and hear the story as observers. They are the field of service, the vineyard, where the disciples minister in the name of the immortal self.

The miracles bear witness to the power of the internal over its own personality and finally become the revelation to all men. The man of soul transforms all things into the likeness of himself and into the fulfillment of his own substance by the miracle of love. By the God-power within him, man quells the tempest, heals the sick, opens the eyes of the blind, casts out evil spirits, and conquers death. The lack of historical evidence to substantiate the miracles attributed to Jesus sustains the mystical conviction that these wonderful works refer to spiritual mysteries. The power of faith over fatality is an essential part of religious doctrine. While Jesus was approaching the house of Jairus, a woman among the throng touched the border of his garment and was healed of a sickness that had afflicted her for twelve years. On this occasion Jesus said to her: "Daughter, be of good comfort: thy faith hath made thee whole; go in peace."

It is the man of soul within the man of flesh who makes all things new. He calms the storms of emotional excess, heals the great sickness which is ignorance, restores the sight of those blinded by materialism, casts out the demons of hate and greed, and overcomes the last great adversary which is the fear of death. Such miracles as these are too intimate and, by their very nature, too secret to be recorded by those historians who are concerned only with physical occurrences. The story of Christianity unfolds through the social changes which have resulted from personal convictions devoutly held and practiced. The effects have their historical dimensions, but the causes cannot be so examined.

Mysticism teaches the alchemy of love. The sorrows and sufferings of mankind originate in false concepts about life and living. When through ignorance or selfishness we violate the good instincts within ourselves, we bear false witness. We think of a perjurer as one who affirms an untruth. In mysticism, the false witness is a betrayer of principles. He testifies by his conduct to a falsehood, and perverts his spiritual resources to his own temporal advantage. The punishment for such an action is the loss of internal peace. When discord takes the place of harmony in the human heart and mind, the resulting disaster is reflected into the body as sickness, into the immediate environment as insecurity, and into the collective social pattern as war and crime. The afflictions which burden us originate in ourselves and not in our world.

The average person desires to be happy, and measures his contentment in terms of health, prosperity, and harmony. Because of the example of the prevailing social-economic fashion, he devotes himself to the fulfillment of those ambitions which he believes will satisfy the yearnings of his soul. Only after disillusionment has revealed the ineffectiveness of the popular conceit does the materialist turn to mysticism for inspiration and guidance. Many Christian sects emphasize the healing and preserving powers of simple and honest faith. Many ailments of the flesh respond more rapidly to an enlargement of consciousness than to the services of a physician. It is unwise, however, to assume that the mere addiction to a noble doctrine will correct bodily infirmities. The average believer is a negative accepter of good principles, and the degree of his devotion is measured by the intensity of his discomfort. Words without works avail little, and the mystic must make an honorable claim to his spiritual resources if he expects to experience their benefits.

The early ministry of Jesus was limited to the region of Galilee, a name which means in Hebrew *rough* or *hilly ground*. The symbolism is obvious; Galilee was a barren place, an appropriate term for the state of materiality. It was inevitable, however, that Jesus would carry his mission to Jerusalem for the final contest between soul and body. Jerusalem was not only the stronghold of orthodox Judaism and the numerous reactionary groups that had appointed themselves custodians of the Torah; it was also the seat of Roman authority in Judea. Behind its ancient walls, sanctified by tradition, were gathered "the powers of this world." It is always necessary that faith shall meet the impact of the grand illusion. Jesus knew beforehand that he should enter Jerusalem in triumph and there be betrayed. His conduct as the world tragedy unfolded is the great mystical example. He kept his own faith, accepting patiently and quietly the insults that were heaped upon him.

Mysticism is a beautiful abstraction as long as we hold it within ourselves. It is not the acceptance of it but the practice of its principles that is the test of courage. It was easy to preach to simple people along the shores of the lake of Galilee, but very difficult to keep the faith in the marts of commerce and the citadels of policy. The fatal journey to Jerusalem described more accurately than we realize the gradual application of conviction to conduct and the consequences. The waiting world, which knows not for what it waits, the world which persecutes the prophets and destroys its saviors, is the vast theater of human activity which glorifies and then crucifies. The ancients symbolized the world as a temple of initiation where each truth seeker and faith finder is tested and proven. Here the man of soul must triumph over the man of body as Jesus did in the garden of Gethsemane. Even the disciples who loved him well could not keep vigil with their Master for one night.

Mysticism is a quiet way of patience and acceptance. There can be no rebellion against the darkness and the children of darkness, because they know not what they do. If there is enough compassion in the heart of the

mystic, he is not resentful or rebellious. This is the final
test of a beautiful faith---that it can endure all things
and suffer all things and continue untroubled, loving
both God and man. If the heart is not strong enough to
do this, the truth seeker is not yet ready to enter Jerusalem.

In its proper time, faith leads the mystic to the
mystical experience. The open heart and mind accept
into themselves the light of God. In that instant all
things become new. Faith is transfigured and becomes
itself a living and radiant power. The substance of
things hoped for is transformed into the substance of
things known. The hope is fulfilled in the fact, and the
mystic no longer sees as through a glass darkly, but
face to face. Without this conscious at-one-ment there
cannot be that strange, deep courage, that unfailing
strength, that complete acceptance of the divine will
which make all other things possible of achievement.
Those who have not experienced the omnipresence of
the love of God will falter when faith is tested. These
are the little ones---the sheep---who still depend upon
the Good Shepherd.

How shall we know faith is strong enough to sustain
the human courage? Each person is aware of his own
spiritual experience. He knows the degree of his own
enlightenment because of the gentle impulses which
slowly but inevitably dominate his way of life. When
there is light in his heart, he understands and accepts
the human problem. He inevitably becomes merciful
and his ways are peaceful and composed even through
adversity. Each of us knows when discord and conten-
tion have been transmuted into peace and harmony.
There is no longer any effort required to control negative instincts. We naturally serve the light and abide in

the light and fulfill ourselves through the works of the light. This is the food of the spirit, and those who eat of it shall no more hunger.

After the betrayal, Jesus was brought before Pilate, who examined him, and, finding no fault, refused to prosecute a just man. Then learning that Jesus was of Galilee, Pilate sent him to Herod, who had jurisdiction over that region. After subjecting Jesus to mockery, Herod returned him to Pilate. This Roman officer, perplexed, called together the chief priests and rulers and also the people of Jerusalem. These were the ones who demanded the death of Jesus, and Pilate washed his hands of the case to signify that the government of Rome would take no part in the proceedings. In this episode Jesus was made to be the victim, not of any recognized government, but of public opinion incited by the priests and prominent citizens. This has always been the fate of spiritual leaders, reformers, and educators. Whatever form the adversary may take, it is always an embodiment of ignorance and selfishness. As far as the world and its policies are involved, the enlightened human being is convicted and sentenced by a jury of the unenlightened.

The soul drama is consummated by the crucifixion. The hero of the world is patient unto death, even the death upon the cross. But in death itself, death is overcome in the mystery of the resurrection. The man of soul rises triumphantly from that bodily sepulchre which is the proper symbol of mortality. Love and faith, indestructible, survive the conspiracies of worldliness. Those who attempt to conquer the world are called despots and tyrants, but those who overcome worldliness in themselves are God's meek who shall inherit the earth. From the nativity in Bethlehem to the ascension on Mt. Olivet, the story of Jesus is the simple and truthful account of the perilous journey from darkness to light.

Each truth seeker, in his own way and according to his own estate, must travel the same road. He must be tempted in the wilderness and must stand firm against the promise of worldly glory. He must minister to those who need, and teach the simple truth of human faith. In the end he must make the great decision, knowing full well that he who saves his life shall lose it, but he who gives his life, sacrificing all to obey the God within, shall have everlasting life. By this wonderful story the ageless truths have been preserved through the centuries to serve and inspire those who hunger and thirst after righteousness. Thus is shown forth how it came to pass that the son of man received into his own heart the ministry of the son of God.

The mystical experience is in no way to be considered historical; it is eternally imminent. It is part of the natural growth of the human creature unfolding the divine plan through its own nature. Yet history bears witness without the historian realizing the full meaning of the records he so patiently assembles. The long, patient struggle of life through the darkness of origin and the twilight of strange and uncertain processes is summarized in the account of one just man. From the beginning the human purpose has struggled against the tyranny of matter. Patiently it has striven, building ever more noble mansions for its soul. From savagery to barbarism and then on to the first dawnings of a civilized way of life, the spirit has impelled the forms which it inhabits. One magnificent life reveals the diversity of living and unfolds the creation through the creature.

At last mind has strengthened the skill to be thoughtful, and the heart has released the power to be loving. These were not always available resources of the human nature. With knowledge has come responsibility, and this, in turn, requires more of wisdom, understanding, and faith. The difficult course of evolution has brought us finally to self-knowing and urges us on to God-knowing. The ways of life that were once the best we knew are no longer satisfying. We have outgrown them, yet we cling desperately to old and familiar concepts and practices. On the threshold of maturity we pause and are afraid. Yet, even as we hesitate, we know that progress is both necessary and inevitable. To the Christian mystic, the life of Jesus clearly indicates the course to be taken. The man of flesh shall decrease as the man of soul increases. A sober and saddened materialism cries out like John the Baptizer, saying: "I baptize with water: but there standeth one among you, whom ye know not; He it is, who coming after me is preferred before me, whose shoe latchet I am not worthy to unloose." The one who stands among us is the man of soul whose way the world has so long denied.

To the mystic, mortal mind, and the vast production thereof, is the prince of this world and his empire. This powerful monarch is described in the sacred writings of the old Egyptians as "the king who ruleth for a day." The will to power has burdened the earth since man first sensed his own significance. It is this will which has dedicated human resources to the interminable task of building a Tower of Babel. But the bricks were made without straw, the work was without the blessing of heaven, and the punishment was a confusion of tongues, of minds, and of hearts. The man of body can no longer control the consequences of his own

ambition. Pride has led to the fall, for thus fell the
angels. There is only one answer: the future of humanity must be placed in the keeping of the man of soul.
There is a nobler and better leader available. This wonderful instructor is the man born of sorrow and experience. His power is expressed through the simple longing
for peace and security. Humanity has outgrown its
ancient policies, and must bestow the new dispensation
out of the hunger of its own heart.

All that is implied by the human hope and faith is
personified in the concept of Jesus. He is the king-priest-
counselor of the secret kingdom of love. He is both the
seeker and the thing sought, the witness and the thing
witnessed. He is earth grown kind from its own pain.
He is man leading man along the way of life. Early
Christian mystics felt impelled to experience the fact of
Jesus within themselves. St. Francis of Assisi became
so completely absorbed in the mystical life of the Master that he received in his hands, feet, and side the
marks of the stigmata. By personal participation in the
life of Jesus, the mystic, not always realizing the full import of his own yearning, reveals the secret of the symbolism. By becoming in every way that he can like
the Master whom he passionately adores, the mystic
achieves the experience of the fact of the great example.
Actually this example is not something separate and
apart from all human understanding.

Jesus stood for humanity and not merely as a symbol
of divinity. Jesus, the son of man, was actually the
embodiment of the human sublime dream. When Jesus
told his disciples that in time they also should do works
greater than his, this was no idle promise. It is as though
our present humanity is a spiritual embryo, and Jesus
one who is already born. As the ideal type of a way of

life for which we are all preparing ourselves, the Master is both the person and the collective of the future. His virtues and powers are those resident in us all, but latent; not dead, but sleeping. The new birth into light is man's awaking to claim his heritage for which he was destined before the beginning of the world. This may appear as a strange interpretation, but it is justified by every line and implication of the Gospels. The hero soul, the savior or redeemer, is always the future self. We have come to that stage of spiritual unfoldment in which we visualize that which is most desirable as the Good Shepherd. Long ago we thought of the hero as the great warrior, the mighty prince, and the conqueror of enemies. But our hearts have grown weary of such dreaming, and we no longer believe that the path of glory leads to peace.

Our own growth is revealed through our concept of the hero. We know him now as one meek and gentle, patient and ever-loving. He wears no crown or armor, but the simple white robe of the dedicated Nazarene. He gathers the children about him, and teaches in simple words and parables that even the most ignorant can understand at least in part. He is patient under adversity, and, having renounced the things of this world, establishes his kingdom, not in the city of his fathers, but in the hearts of his fellow men. Can we not understand that this concept is ourselves? It is our story and our gradual awakening into a world of gentle and beautiful realities. We respect and venerate the life and teachings of Jesus because they reveal our own most sacred hopes and most precious convictions. He is ourselves after we have escaped certain limitations which yet appear difficult.

To those still living under the old dispensation it seems impossible that faith can take the place of force in the guidance of human affairs. We have inherited an environment of collective pressures which seem to oppose all our gentler instincts. We feel that we must fight our way to the securities we seek, and defend with every resource at our disposal the goods we have accumulated. To depart from this code is to be convicted of impractical idealism. When reviewing the story of the mortal strife, we point to certain evidences of progress, and comfort ourselves with the thought that the end justifies the means. The good things we now enjoy have been bought at a terrible price. We have advanced by the long and difficult road of mortal pain. Why, then, do we insist so emphatically that our policies are above improvement?

Faith itself is a powerful constructive force which accomplishes its ends by natural and gentle means. Perhaps the human race is now old enough to appreciate and sad enough to accept a positive philosophy of growth. There is no proof that mysticism has failed, but abundant proof that materialism is impractical. The man of soul is the governor of the man of flesh by divine right. As the Greeks expressed it, there is a universal law that inferiors shall be ruled by superiors. The soul is superior to the body, and the internal life of man is superior to his external activities. To release soul power through the administrative instruments of civilization is to transform, transmute, and regenerate these instruments. Why do we so patiently and consistently labor against our own welfare, serving the prince of this world with a devotion that merits a better cause?

Humanity is being drawn by an irresistible power toward a great decision. We willingly accept the fact of progress. We know that we have unfolded from a primitive condition to our present state. Is there any reason to suppose that we shall not continue to grow? In what direction is Nature leading us forward? Is scientific progress on a physical level all that lies ahead? Is it man himself or merely the products of his ingenuity to which the law of evolution is now applicable? Is the human mind to be sacrificed to its own productions and the human heart to be satisfied with its worldly attachments? History tells us that all the works of man are perishable. It is only man himself who is imperishable.

Mysticism is dedicated to the release of the human being from bondage to his own accomplishments. It reveals the larger dignity of the self that stands in the midst of the circumstances which it engenders. Man's path is not only forward, but also upward; not only into the future, but also toward the light. What does it profit a man if he accomplish worldly success and honor but has no peace or contentment in his own heart? The mystic is not opposed to science or philosophy or even economics so long as these productions of human skill are instruments of positive soul growth. It is not use but abuse which betrays the common good. Knowledge ensouled is the servant of God, but without spiritual grace it is the instrument of death. As the mind creates the body of learning, the heart must bestow that inner beauty by which learning becomes gracious and gentle.

We learn also from history that there have always been a few who were born out of time. These children of the future were not poor visionaries resolved to create artificial worlds of their own; they were the sons of towardness or, as one mystic called them, "heralds of the dawn." In their lives was revealed the rising of the sun of truth. They bore witness to convictions that will one day guide the human effort. These better men embodied that which is better in all men. In our hearts we honor those who reveal through their conduct the richness of the human potential. We may not understand their thoughts or share their vision, but deep within ourselves we are grateful that they lived.

The man of Syria was not the only wonderful example of spiritual conviction who has dwelt among us, but he is more familiar to us than those of other lands. Although we know little of the life of Jesus, he has become the embodiment of a solid spiritual conviction. For more than fifteen centuries kings have been crowned in his name and governors have taken oath of office upon his book. We have given him all worldly honors, and in every community there are shrines dedicated in his name and to his work. To Christendom, this man is the King of Kings and the Prince of Peace. In spite of all this we live in strife and discord, each man fearing his neighbor, and nations poised on the brink of war.

Mysticism has a simple explanation for this strange and dramatic inconsistency. Our faith is still historical. Religion is part of our environment, and we participate in it as we share other utilities and advantages. Someway we believe that the church is in the keeping of its ministers and priests and they are the ones who must bring about its final triumph, in which we will share and by which we shall benefit. Christianity is not a kind of climate to be accepted and adapted to our own inclinations. We cannot become wise by going to school, or Christians simply by going to church. A nominally Christian civilization gains from its affiliations only what it bestows from its own consciousness. Without the mystical experience of religion, faith remains negative and sterile. Theology is brought to us by the clergy, but religion comes through us from the source of good within our hearts. We must realize that we can be drowned in a sea of faith and die faithless unless we personally experience the presence of God.

The Christian faith has always been essentially mystical. It never appealed directly to the scholar, the sage, or the philosopher. It made no effort to compete with the workings of the mind or to advance the horizons of material progress. This has been held against Christianity by most intellectuals and, to a degree, the criticism appears just. The greater difficulty arose, however, when the Christian faith became involved in the political policies of nations and sought to establish its own authority. By this action it sold its birthright for a bowl of pottage. It set for its followers an unfortunate example by justifying the concept that the church was a material organization requiring material support and imposing material regulations upon its followers. This substitution of earthly ambitions for spiritual aspirations compromised the mystical side of the doctrine.

Gentle meditation upon the life and ministry of Jesus naturally justifies and encourages the kindliness and charity which is within all of us. At first we may only admire and respect, but that which so enlarges and justifies our admiration gradually intensifies our resolution to do likewise. As the courage of a good faith strengthens conduct, we become immediately and intimately aware of the importance of living. The change in ourselves rejoices our own hearts and transforms us from static followers of creeds to dynamic servants of principles. Life is only important when it has high purpose. With hope, faith, and love in our hearts guiding our minds and hands, we cannot fail, and we serve a cause that cannot fail.

ANTIQUE JEWEL DEPICTING THE GOOD SHEPHERD

Chapter Four

THE MINISTRY OF JESUS

All inspired spiritual leaders bestow upon those who come after them a threefold heritage. There is always the good example, the inspired teaching, and the communion, or assembly. The life of Jesus, as preserved in the Gospels, constitutes the good example and is familiar to Christians throughout the world. The Master left no writings of his own, but his sayings, sermons, and parables are preserved in the books attributed to the four Evangelists. The communion, which began with the disciples of the apostles, finally became the Christian Church, the numerous denominations of which have vast followings. To the mystic, each of the parts of the Christian dispensation has a special meaning and significance as an experience of consciousness.

We have already emphasized that mysticism is not a creed, but a quality of spiritual apperception. Mystics

82

of all religious groups honor and respect the life and teachings of Jesus even though they prefer their own teachers and prophets. One of the proofs of man's maturing soul-nature is his increasing appreciation of integrity whenever and wherever it appears. Love of truth brings peace, and when our devotion to God is stronger than our addiction to cults, there will be no more private intolerance and public religious strife. Love overcomes, one by one, the false obstacles which divide human hearts. By simple and gracious action alone, we relieve ourselves and others of many unhappy experiences.

The ministry of Jesus covers that brief period between his baptism by John and his death on Calvary. The outstanding policy which dominated the ministry was freedom from prevailing prejudices and arbitrary conventions. Jesus did not proclaim his ministry to those occupying positions of privilege or authority. He chose the unlearned in preference to those wise in their own conceits. He seems to have known the peculiar difficulties which beset the minds of influential persons who have apparently succeeded without benefit of truth. One of the problems of today is the ponderous structure of opinion which has no solid ethical foundation. To the average person it seems impossible that the accumulated lore which passes for knowledge can be comparatively valueless. We hasten to embrace that which has been made respectable by general acceptance, and then wonder why we share in the common disaster.

Jesus taught that it was easier for a camel to pass through a needle's eye than for a rich man to enter heaven. We have all assumed that in this analogy riches implied only physical possessions. There are other kinds of material wealth, not the least of which is the belief in the abundance of our intellectual resources. To believe that we *are* because we *have* is false, regardless of the nature of the goods. The smug intellectualist is not only wise in his own conceits, but considers himself richly endowed with priceless mental assets. Worldly wisdom is admired as a form of wealth because it bestows a sense of superiority and that pride which comes before a fall.

The reformation of human conduct depends more upon the cleansing of the mind of illusions and delusions than upon new instruction. It is man himself who has changed the living temple of his spirit into a house of merchandise. When Jesus called the children to him, he reminded his disciples that of such was the kingdom of heaven. As a mystic he taught what Herbert Spencer, the English philosopher, expressed in more scientific terms. Spencer defined the involutionary processes of Nature, by which life becomes immersed in form, as a motion from unity to diversity or from simplicity to complexity. He then described evolution, or the release of life from form, as a motion from diversity to unity or from complexity to simplicity. Modern intellectualism is almost completely frustrated by its own heterogeneity. Direct action has become the exception rather than the rule. The need for reintegration is evident in private lives and public projects.

The seat of direct action is within man and not in the systems he has created. At the present time the human mind is released from false values by a process we call disillusionment. This detachment is only possible as the result of some major catastrophe, internal or social. We reject prevailing patterns only when we are convinced that they are inadequate or actually destructive. Most mystics have turned from worldliness because it betrayed the confidence bestowed upon its concepts and practices. Thus, by a direct action of the will, the consciousness rejected traditional policies. By this very action it acknowledged a state of unknowing. A decision was made, and destiny was returned to the keeping of the divine will. Simple faith in the availability of God's love and protection when experienced as a personal certainty is the first genuine religious action.

Calling his disciples from among fishermen and peasants, Jesus revealed the peculiar purpose of his work. He made no effort to expound a strange doctrine of heavenly mysteries, but through his parables gave them the keys to a wonderful kingdom. Faith is like the mustard seed which, finding good ground, grows into a great "tree." It is not necessary for the teacher to constantly guide and guard the growth of faith; the mystery unfolds from within itself if the soil be proper. To build upon simple things which can be known in the heart is to build well and to place a secure foundation beneath our dreams and aspirations. We all have the tendency to make simple things difficult, but the spirit that abides within us achieves its own ends by making all difficult things simple.

Mysticism as an internal experience must be supported by an appropriate pattern of personal conduct. The physical body is the immediate environment of the soul. We are all inclined to believe that a harmonious environment contributes to peace of mind and graciousness of conduct. Mystics live simply because they feel that pretensions and temporal ambitions are likely to disturb the body and its functions. The corporeal considerations are not ignored or rejected. We gain nothing by denying facts or attempting to distort them to conform with unreasonable opinions. The personality requires work, rest, and recreation, and to disregard these natural requirements is to endanger the emotional and mental powers. Whatever disturbs tranquillity, causing stress, fear, worry or anxiety, operates contrary to well-being. Devotion to mysticism, therefore, includes the moderation of all excesses and the conservation of all resources.

Pressures distort gentle feelings and instincts and obscure spiritual vision. We cannot serve both error and truth at the same time; we must relinquish one in order to cultivate the other. Growth is a direct and positive process once we are dedicated to principles. We overcome vice, not by locking ourselves in mortal combat with our faults, but by emphasizing quietly and patiently the good qualities of our dispositions. Growth is not a desperate struggle to improve, but a kindly unfoldment of the best of our native qualities. Once we have decided to seek the kingdom of heaven, we dedicate all of ourselves to the quest. Such unity of purpose can be attained only by complete internal relaxation. We are sustained by motive rather than by effort. Right motive censors both heart and mind and reveals the level of sincerity on which we are functioning.

Destructive intensities reveal ulterior motives, and these in turn limit growth.* It is quite possible to glamorize selfishness and ambition until they appear meritorious. It is no safer to be proud of wisdom than to be proud of ignorance. To cultivate the attributes of spirituality in order to satisfy frustrated ambitions or to make an otherwise useless life appear useful is to invite disaster; yet religion has always served as an outlet for the neurotic. The halt, the lame, and the blind have demanded the consolation of their faith, but have contributed little of strength or integrity to the sects which they have joined. In mysticism it is what we give and not what we gain that determines spiritual progress.

With only a sincere faith to guide our hearts and minds, we must live the doctrines which we claim to believe. It is one thing to affirm the reality of good and our devotion thereto, and quite another matter to return good for evil on a particular occasion. The affirmation is without merit, for it may be nothing more than an intellectual platitude. Strangely enough, we can affirm and even defend with skill and courage that which we affirm and still be without faith. But when, with no hope of profit to ourselves and without consideration for our own injured feelings, we naturally and instinctively do good to those who despitefully use us, we are performing the works of faith and love. Wherever it occurs that religious teachings, themselves honorable and reasonable, have seemed to fail or have led to intolerance, it is usually the believer and not the belief that is to blame. No doctrine can be devised that cannot be perverted or corrupted. Those who bear false witness to a noble and beautiful teaching are guilty of a serious fault.

The example of the life of the great spiritual teacher strengthens our determination to follow in his footsteps. Jesus said to his disciples: "If ye love me, keep my commandments." (St. John, 14:15) In the following chapter, verse 12, the Master then states his doctrine: "This is my commandment, that ye love one another, as I have loved you." To keep the commandments can only mean to act in conformity with the spirit of the instruction. A nominal Christian world has affirmed the divinity of Jesus and pays homage to his ministry, but to what degree has it actually kept his commandments? Does the average persistent churchgoer love

God with all his heart and all his soul and love his neighbor as himself? If so, how shall we explain the tragedy, compounded from the elements of selfishness, ambition, hate, and suspicion, which burdens humankind? I have known many well-intentioned persons who claimed to be sincere and devout. These same ones have nursed their grievances, perpetuated their animosities, and have not found it in their hearts to forget, to forgive, or to understand the faults of others. To the mystic there can be no consolation in faith apart from the commandments of faith.

The first step toward truth is to cleanse the heart and mind of all grievances. This is not only a moral duty, but also an essential element in the mystical experience. The embittered, the disillusioned, the cynical, and the self-pitying can never know the blessings of the heavenly power. Even while such unpleasant persons are praying for release from their miseries, they are making that release impossible by their own conduct. The Comforter, whose coming is promised by the Scriptures, can be interpreted as the spirit of peace that abides with those who have renounced their own negative thoughts and emotions.

The burden of the old dispensation is revealed through the Ten Commandments. The finger of the Lord traced in letters of fire upon the sapphire tablets the law for Israel. Amidst the clouds and lightning of Sinai, Adonai proclaimed the Torah through a series of admonitions, most of which commenced with the words: "Thou shalt not . . ." Jesus brought the new dispensation to his disciples and followers in a different way. He gathered them about him and instructed them in gentle and simple words. In The First Epistle General of John, the teachings of the Master are beautifully summarized: "There is no fear in love; but perfect love casteth out fear: because fear hath torment. He that feareth is not made perfect in love.

"We love him, because he first loved us.

"If a man say, I love God, and hateth his brother, he is a liar: but he that loveth not his brother whom he hath seen, how can he love God whom he hath not seen?

"And this commandment have we from him, That he who loveth God love his brother also."

According to the tenets of mysticism, love perfects law by ensouling it with the grace of the spirit. Where there are many laws without love, there is much lawlessness, but when love abides in the heart, there is slight need for rules and regulations. We have attempted for thousands of years to govern men by imposing restrictions upon their conduct, yet as Solon, the Athenian legislator, so wisely remarked: "Legal codes are like the web of the spider, which captures small insects, but allows stronger creatures to break through and escape." It is the humanity within man which must ultimately triumph over man's inhumanity to man. Why, then, do we insist that the teachings of Jesus cannot be applied to the management of world affairs? Is the mystic merely a visionary or is he a good man strengthened by vision? Laws are imposed upon society, but love grows within the human heart and, by changing the man, redeems the nation.

In an age dedicated to scientific skepticism, the average person has slight appreciation of spiritual values. He does not realize that behind and beneath the complex confusion of contemporary civilization lies one simple dilemma. The struggle of the ages, symbolized by the rise and fall of cultures, is the conflict between faith and fear. Faith is a uniting force, and fear a dividing force. Through faith we are brought together in a communion of noble purposes. By fear we are separated, each attempting to insure his own survival by exploiting others. Until faith becomes as natural, normal, and acceptable to the human being as are the fears which now beset him, neither the individual nor the group can experience lasting peace or security. We are impoverished by our fears, even as we are enriched by our faith. Enduring progress is made possible by faith in the future. Personal growth is justified by faith in ourselves, and the reformation of our institutions must bear witness to our faith in humanity.

Faith is not sustained by the visible works of man under existing conditions. We must, therefore, depend upon the increasing light within ourselves for the strength of our convictions. Without love for God, there can be no sufficient faith. Thus faith and love are inseparable and are together the sure foundation for a good hope. We cannot accomplish faith by a mere determination. If we would receive the consolation of the spirit, we must abide together in peace. The simple code of personal relationship taught by Jesus is therefore a little key to a great mystery. Faith is an acceptance of things unknown, but not in substance unknowable. Only by means of a spiritual integration of his own personality can the truth seeker experience the fact of reality.

As the embodiment of the mystical tradition, Jesus reveals the journey of the soul's awakening. In him, strength and humility were wonderfully mingled. He fulfilled his mission with a quiet courage, yet in his nature there was no bitterness or resentment or animosity. He understood the universal plan so well that he was no longer disturbed by the frailties of human nature or the inconsistencies of human conduct. To love those who despitefully use us requires more of understanding than is usually available. It is true, however, of us all that we dislike most that which we understand least. It is difficult to really know and not be kind, even as it is difficult to be ignorant and not be unkind. Our estimations of others are based upon the level of consciousness which we have achieved through internal growth.

The mystic experiences a universe that is completely acceptable to his consciousness. This does not mean that he is content to exist without further self-improvement. He knows in his heart that a future of infinite opportunity unfolds before him inviting him to grow and earn his spiritual heritage. But he accepts fact with faith, and knows that at any given moment of universal time each human being is in the proper place which he has earned for himself. Each is doing the best he can according to what he is and what he knows. Each is growing and learning through experience, and each is evolving and unfolding the divine powers which are latent within him. There is no merit in wondering why growth is not more rapid or virtues so slow in maturing. There is no cause for resentment because others treat us badly or fail to agree with our conclusion or opinion. We walk together in twilight, and if one seems to be wiser than another it is because "in the world of the blind, the one-eyed man is king."

Once we accept the divine plan without reservation or objection, we experience a realization of peace. We no longer struggle against inevitables, but work with them as good and faithful servants. Those who most need this quietude within themselves are not always of a mind to meet its requirements. We spend too much time defending our right to be unhappy and blaming others for our nontranquillity. The mystic has outgrown completely the illusion of an exterior cause for an interior disaster. He knows that his own false estimates, mistaken judgments, and immature opinions are responsible for his sorrows. The more we expect from others, the more we open ourselves to disappointment; the more we demand of others, the less likely it is that we shall experience contentment. It would be difficult, indeed, to destroy the composure of those who give all of themselves and require nothing in return. Epicurus, the philosopher, once said: "He is richest whose needs are fewest." This is a true but not a popular aphorism.

The more we are sustained by internal strength, the less we demand of life around us. Each must keep his happiness in his own name. No man is so rich or powerful that he can hire another to sleep for him or to eat for him. Each must perform the essential requirements of survival, and this is true of the inner life as well. He is badly served who depends upon the doctor, the lawyer, and the priest for his internal security. Because we are ignorant, we hire experts, and because we hire experts, we are content to remain ignorant. It makes little difference whether we lean for support upon a learned man or upon a prevailing and popular concept about living. To depend for strength upon that which is not ourselves is folly. The moment we seek counsel we admit our own ignorance, and this admission should move us to improve ourselves.

Unfortunately, we ask many questions for which there are no useful answers and accumulate information which will never be serviceable. Thus, there is a quantity of so-called knowledge which only burdens the mind without comforting the spirit. Nature does not require that any of its creatures know more than they can understand or use faculties for their salvation which they do not possess. The benefits of the mystical experience are available to all and at all times through the direct act of faith. It would seem that the inner awareness of God conveys an overknowledge, not of particulars but of principles, not of parts but of wholeness. This overknowledge is accompanied by a quiet contentment, whereas worldly knowledge usually leads to further and larger dissatisfaction.

It is difficult to explain such a term as *knowledge of wholeness*. The Greek mystics defined it as "participation in causes," by which they meant *soul-awareness of the divine plan*. As the intent and purpose of God is inwardly known, the consciousness is filled with a wonderful understanding that cannot be defined. Some have claimed to possess this understanding, and others to have been possessed by it. Such claims mean nothing unless they are sustained by an appropriate improvement of character. No one can actually experience internal illumination and not reveal this enlargement of understanding in daily living. Growth is a positive process and bears witness to itself. We know that improvement is real when it refines and ennobles human character.

The lives of mystics prove the victory of internal light over internal darkness. The soul that is troubled is in darkness, for light brings with it a complete resignation to the divine will. There is a moment of strange, indescribable silence when it seems that all motions of the world cease. In that instant the currents of consciousness are reversed. It is much like the reversal of the blood circulation which takes place at physical birth. It is reported in the sacred writings of most religions

that the birth of the Messiah is accompanied by wonders. All Nature unites to pay homage to the child of
heaven. The spiritual chemistry of the advent cannot
be adequately described in words. The divine self rises
victoriously from the not-self. The God power within
comes into its kingdom, and the prince of this world and
his legions are baffled. Actually, it is by this mystery
that the human being becomes a person and assumes
the obligation of enlightened selfhood. The man of
soul is in the world, but not of it. He becomes intuitively
aware of his own place in the divine plan. He accepts
this place and fulfills its requirements. We are in darkness as long as we are negative and the world in which
we live is positive. The mystical experience reveals the
eternal truth that consciousness is positive, and to it
all environments are negative.

All the world is seeking internal peace. Like happiness, peace cannot be required or demanded, nor can it
be accomplished by direct effort of the will. Internal
security is a consequence and not a cause of human
unfoldment. It is available only to those who have first
experienced the simple power of faith. If we are to
know, we must first be still, and there can be no silence
where there is discord. Enlightened love, by overcom-
ing confusion, makes possible the miracle of stillness.
It is said in Genesis that the Lord walked in the garden
in the coolness of the evening. Our lives are like gardens,
but if we neglect these gardens, they are no longer
beautiful. Weeds destroy the flowering growth until
we find no pleasure in the forlorn surroundings. If
each keeps his garden faithfully, he shall find repose
there after the hours of labor, and, perchance, come
face to face with the Great Gardener.

Jesus taught by example the way of spiritual union. He gave the laws by which the tranquillity of the inner nature is available to all who honestly and earnestly seek truth. Even though generation after generation of human beings rejects or ignores the good example, the facts remain unchanged. For numberless reasons that appear sufficient, we may refuse to accept the mystical concept, but until we face reality and walk the ageless path, there is no end to suffering. We cannot change the universal plan for our redemption; we must change ourselves to meet the requirements of that plan. It sometimes seems that we are asked to sacrifice too much for something that we cannot understand, but as we grow we realize that all we renounce is our sovereign right to be miserable.

The second part of the ministry of Jesus relates to the instructions and teachings. These include the sermons and parables and words spoken on various occasions. The teachings of the Master are remarkable for the association which they imply between God and Jesus. Taken literally, these utterances have strengthened the conviction that the Master claimed to be the only begotten son of the universal Deity. Some sects have gone so far as to teach that the Godhead was incarnated in Jesus, although such an extreme belief is not justified by the Biblical text. When Philip asked Jesus to reveal to the disciples the heavenly Father, the Master answered him: "Believest thou not that I am in the Father, and the Father in me? The words that I speak unto you I speak not of myself: but the Father that dwelleth in me, he doeth the works."

Such a statement as this is completely meaningful only to the mystic, who has experienced the immanence of the divine power. In mysticism, God is apperceptively known, not as a vast sovereignty, but as an all-pervading and ever-present quality. There is no longer an immeasurable interval between the human need and the divine supply. God is the ever-present help no farther from us than the strength of our own faith. The heart does not rejoice in honors or dignities, nor does it acknowledge differences of estate. It accepts the divine presence as parent, lover, brother, and friend. If it seems that this attitude compromises the temporal glory of God, it destroys only an image, and releases Deity from the dimensions imposed upon his glory by mortal ignorance.

The power that is mindful of each sparrow's fall and which manifests itself in the beauty of all things great and small cannot be personally experienced as a god of wrath or of vengeance or as a mighty king ruling despotically from a distant throne above the firmament. The divine presence is revealed wherever living things unfold their hidden wonders. Meditation upon the mystery of the eternal Father ends inevitably in the revelation of the omnipresence of Deity. In God we live and move and have our being; we are part of him, and he is all of us. Apart from him there is no life, no hope, and no dream. How then, shall we present this grateful worship that cannot be directed toward heaven above or toward the earth below? It flows from us toward life, and the blessings everywhere abundant return to us. The mystic lives constantly in the realization of ever-present divine strength. He knows himself to be a radiant spark within the divine flame. He understands also that his life is not his own, but a universal life expressing through him. This life is the heavenly Father of the earthly man, and it is always this Father "that doeth the work."

The skeptic may say that this experience of identity with God is merely a form of the divinity complex. Yet, when this complex occurs in pathological cases of mental unbalance, it does not result in a state of mystical identity. The aspiring human soul becoming aware of its eternal birthright is not proud or self-satisfied or self-centered as the result. Mystics are the humblest and simplest of persons and their hearts are filled with gratitude. They are happy and content to regard themselves as the children of an all-loving parent. They ask no more than to serve and obey. In this case, obedience is not given because it is required, but because the love of God allows no alternative. Those whom we love we protect, and upon them we bestow all that we have and all that we are. How much more, then, does this normal human instinct find its fulfillment in the realization of the divine presence?

Jesus told his disciples that he came to bear witness of the love of the Father. It was the privilege of good men to live by the law of life. If they did so, they also bore witness. In this way, religion was given a fuller meaning. We worship according to the dictates of our own hearts and serve the truths we honor. As we grow and unfold the mystical divinity within ourselves, it seems to speak to our hearts and minds. The teaching that comes from within ourselves is substantially the Sermon on the Mount. Thus Jesus, as the man of soul in each of us, reveals his ministry through our own unfoldment. The message spoken from our hearts is gentle and kindly and strangely detached from the confusion of our external lives. From our own belongings and seekings and hopings we fashion a mystical mood or reverie. The mood fulfills itself, receiving a sustaining testimony from the innermost parts of our being. God enters our lives

as a well-loved friend with whom we share our worldly
goods and our heavenly aspirations. There is no need
for herald angels or inspired interpreters. We go to our
Father and we ask his help and his guidance, certain
of his wisdom and love because we are his children
and this is our natural right.

Advanced mystics have so unfolded their own apperceptive powers that sometimes they experience a
complete identity with God through rapture or ecstasy.
All sense of separateness or of existence apart from God
is dissolved in an extraordinary quality of aspiration. In
that moment the mystic can exclaim with complete
certainty: "The Father and I are one." No word can
describe or thought unfold the mystery of divine union.
The mystic feels himself sharing both the unity and
diversity of the universal power. He contracts with it
into a center of absolute peace, and expands with it
toward a circumference of absolute differentiation. In
both contraction and expansion he is sharing in the
qualities of the sovereign good. He experiences also the
infinite tenderness of the divine mind, its wisdom and
love, and, to a degree at least, knows the sorrow of
heaven---the very pain of God that was made flesh for
the redemption of the ages.

Such exaltations of the spirit, like the vision of St.
John on Patmos, are not of long duration. It seems as
though man would be dissolved utterly did he not escape back into the narrow chambers of mortality. But
when such a one returns to his old way of life, something of God is with him and remains forever. One who
has been made new in faith returns to the mortal world
with clearer vision and deeper understanding. There
is no longer any need to struggle against limitations and
temptations, for how can a man be tempted who has

known the truth? Even those who have gone but a little way along the mystic path have no desire to return except to serve others. Jesus attempted to reveal to his disciples the experience of mysticism. He sought to strengthen them for the work which they should do after he was gone. He knew that only from within themselves could they find security and courage. Unfortunately, they understood only in part and therefore were but partly consoled. Through the long centuries, those of little faith interpreted away the true mystery of transubstantiation. They could not understand the man who, breaking the bread, told them it was his body, and sharing the wine, told them it was his blood.

Most of those who have rejected the Christian faith have refused to accept an outer form and have not realized the inner part. Is not a good man merely an embodiment of goodness, and a wise man the instrument of wisdom? Are goodness and wisdom bound into the chemistry of creatures? Do we give life to the children we bear or are we merely channels of an eternal life? Is the love in our hearts actually our own or is it a manifestation of a universal emotion? Have we any powers, faculties, perceptions, or instincts that do not originate in the spiritual source of existence? We may reveal and release, we may bind and loose, but only because we have been endowed with potentials which we are privileged to transform into perfect powers. If man is part of the Infinite, then his mind shares in the Infinite mind, and his heart in the Infinite heart. Thus we bear witness, and, in a strange way, those who see us behold the invisible agent which created us. The Father is made manifest in his works and is especially revealed through his beloved son, who symbolizes humanity itself.

Jesus is the prototype of the enlightened human being. The word is made flesh in man, and made soul
through the unfoldment of man. Jesus promised his
disciples that the time would come when they should
perform works greater than his. This is the message of
the one who has seen to those who have not yet seen.
The great teachers are the Elder Brothers bearing witness to the inevitable destiny of a God-ensouled creation. Can we deny this without denying the testimony
of our senses, the intuition of our hearts, and the convictions of our minds? And if we do deny it, what have
we accomplished but the complete impoverishment of
ourselves? Jesus taught a natural and simple growing-
up in the light of truth. He used the parables to emphasize how Nature is forever testifying to the divine plan.
Everywhere the way of heaven is revealed, but there
are none so blind as those who will not see or cannot
see because their sight has been destroyed by false
doctrines.

From the ministry naturally developed the congregation, or the assembly of believers, which we know as
the Church. Originally, simple and pious men and wom-
en gathered in quiet places to worship in secret. Later,
churches and cathedrals were built, and the first ecclesia
expanded to become the House of Christendom. Permanent religious institutions always fulfill a twofold
purpose. They spread the teachings in a social system
which seems to require at least a degree of physical
organization. This material consideration, unfortunately, has been given precedence. Mystically understood, the
assembly represents the nucleus of the spiritual kingdom.

As the seed of the soul is sown in the heart of man
for his salvation, so the congregation is the collective
seed sown in the structure of society for the improve-

ment of all men. The seed-power of God is strengthened when several are united by one conviction. In spiritual union there is divine strength, and in united effort there is formed a new body which becomes the vehicle for the incarnation of the soul of the faith. To function in a world of form, divine principles must take form and exist in our midst, appearing like ourselves and subject to our limitations.

Organized Christianity recognized and accepted the essential fact of the mystical experience, but only within its own communion. As the self-appointed custodian of human salvation, theology reserved to itself the power of final decision in all religious matters. It condemned unconditionally those whose search for inner enlightenment led them away from the restrictions imposed by orthodoxy. This restraint upon the natural instincts of the heart and mind divided the congregation and resulted in schisms. The mystic could not accept the concept that a mortal institution could be legitimately empowered to dictate the policies of human salvation. The intimate association between God and man was beyond the keeping of the clergy.

The remnants of mystical sects which had survived from earlier times drew to themselves many earnest believers who had rejected what seemed to them a perversion of original Christianity. These dissenters became the heretics against which the Church turned its militant arm. Forced into secrecy by persecution, the mystics created their own communion, appointed ministers from among themselves, and were for centuries the custodians of an esoteric Christianity. The Courts of Love of the Troubadours and the Hidden Church of the Holy Grail were sincere attempts to restore the true ecclesia of Jesus and his disciples. Many strange cults, clothing their doctrines in mysterious symbols, bore witness to this mystical devotion.

After the Reformation, there is little evidence of mysticism in the descent of the Protestant sects. These were devoted largely to the defense of their own protests and their dogged devotion to their own orthodoxies. Almost immediately the mystics separated themselves from the reformed groups and emerged as minor orders, tolerated but resented. The dominant divisions of the faith, while acknowledging the possibility of the personal experience of God, have never clarified for their members either the means or the end involved in the concept of spiritual union. To the average person of today, mysticism is only a term bestowed upon a condition of internal conviction of dubious authenticity. It does not occur to the average worshiper that personal illumination is what one alchemist quaintly described as "the true entrance to the shut palace of the King."

The living church is the congregation and not the building in which it is housed. Like the kingdom of God, the ecclesia is not of this world, and that which exists here can be only a symbol. It is a mistake to accept the symbol as the reality, even as it is wrong to worship an image instead of the principle for which it stands. The substitution in the mind of idols for ideals has transformed a way of redemption into a confusion of creeds. Insidiously, this substitution has influenced the entire course of human civilization. We have become content to sacrifice principles and to devote our resources to the glorification of our own material accomplishments.

Those who have attained to the spirit of mysticism accept the religions of the world as they accept all other manifestations of human evolution. The heavenly Father whom they serve is in every place and is available to the devout of all beliefs. There can be no theological prejudices on the level of natural religion. The mosque, the temple, the shrine, the synagogue, and the cathedral were built by men seeking truth. Those who understand the human heart enter all these places with reverence, for they are sanctified to the God of ages. Wherever we are, we worship according to whatever we are. Faith is a quality beyond time and place, but immediately available in all times and in all places. We never become so righteous that we are justified in persecuting what we regard as lack of wisdom.

As love brings understanding, so the heart doctrine emphasizes the good which has inspired all the honorable works and dreams of mankind. Finally, there can be no temple but the world itself, which is the Everlasting House and the living sanctuary. Until such time as this mystery is completely known in the soul, we increase in grace by broadening the foundations of faith. To the mechanist, the universe is a machine; to the vitalist, a magnificent living organism; to the idealist, the manifestation of the universal mind; and to the mystic, the eternal sanctuary. Each sees according to the light within himself. Each is right as far as his vision goes, and no one sees perfectly. Even the mystic is continuing to expand the God consciousness within him, and as he becomes more enlightened he will comprehend many things now concealed behind the veil which protects the Holy of Holies.

Jesus told his disciples that there were other sheep not of his fold, but he also promised them that the day would come when there would be one sheepfold and one shepherd. This has been interpreted to mean that the Christian dispensation was predestined to be the

religion of all men. Perhaps a quality of faith and not
a sect was implied. Actually, there is only one spiritual
conviction and, although it has been called by many
names, it is above and beyond creedal limitations. The
natural religion of mankind is revealed through the instincts to love, to hope, and to serve. When these generous impulses direct human activities, humanity is one
congregation united in truth rather than by allegiance
to a name. Among the Greeks, the word *sheepfold*
was applied to a place of initiation into the mysteries
of religion. Those who had accepted the religious life
were called the sheep, and their masters and instructor-
priests were called shepherds. This seems to be the implication which Jesus intended to convey. His disciples,
like the Greek mystae, had been accepted into the circle
of the illumined. They had received instructions and
had assumed the obligations inherent in the doctrine.
They had offered themselves to the service of God, and
acknowledged Jesus as their Good Shepherd.

Many of the early Christian forms and symbols were
derived from older religions. We cannot understand
these references and allusions unless we have some
knowledge of their source and earlier meanings. In the
Eleusinian Mysteries performed in ancient Attica, those
passing through the lower grades successfully were
termed *mystae,* and those who had completed the higher grades were referred to as *epoptae.* The mystae were
permitted to advance to the veil which divided the inner
parts of the sanctuary from the larger chambers of re-
ception. This was the grade of faith, for the truth seeker
was allowed to glimpse the adytum only through a veil.
He must accept the reality of things unseen and the
substance of things hoped for. It was reserved for the
epoptae to part the veil and behold the mystery face

to face. It is evident from I. Corinthians, 13:12 that St. Paul was aware of the Greek symbolism.

If the love of God is to be perfectly manifested among men, the ecclesia, or congregation, must make the proper claim by preparing the way. The immaculate conception has many interpretations. To the mystic it means that the Logos, or Word, made flesh, must have a pure body, and that body is the pledge, or testimony, prepared by the Elect. The proof that man is ready to accept the mystery of redemption is witnessed through his works. Those who live together in concord, having fellowship one with another, those who work together, thinking not of themselves but of the common good, and those who pray together, loving God with a single and simple devotion, unite to form the living Grail, the cup which is to receive the blood of the King. This is the mystical sacrament so beautifully described in the story of Parsifal. The knights of the Grail were dedicated to the service of the voice and the power that came from the cup which represented the bleeding heart of heaven.

It is the privilege of the Christian communion to fufill the destiny for which it was intended. Before this is possible, however, it must re-experience the mystical sacrament. We are preserved, not by continued devotion to creeds, but by the expansion and release of the living power of an illumined faith. As man grows in grace from within himself, so the congregation must receive into its heart those invisible energies of God which are said to descend upon the high altar with its mystical symbols and adornments. All that is real in religion is to be known only by the single faculty of the soul. As the light of the sun ripens the harvest, so the light of God, shining upon the congregation, ripens the inner life of man, making it fruitful as the Lord has required.

The ministry of Jesus fulfilled the three parts of the revelation of the divine will. To the outer man, it gave the example of right living; to the intellectual nature, it brought the glad tidings of the right use of faculties and energies; to the human heart, it gave the communion of souls and the fulfillment of all doctrines by the power of love. There can be no fellowship in the spirit, no consolation in the faith unless we work together. As we give of ourselves unselfishly, in like measure we receive. In this way, the ecclesia assumes a new significance. Through it, that which we claim is revealed and made known and justified. The church is not a place where we go to seek God, but the assembly of those who become conscious channels and dedicated instruments of the dissemination of the divine nature. The whole congregation is one priest---not a mediator, but a witness to the inevitable. We assemble, not to gain, but to give, becoming one body awaiting ensoulment.

When each one knows that it is possible for him to become the hands and feet of truth, he will fulfill that which his Creator has ordained. Until then he is apprenticed to his conceits, and serves only that which shall perish away. Mysticism not only makes all things real, but all good works immediate. There are no longer times and places; only that which is necessary and the natural impulse to fulfill the need. The mind recognizes the difficulties of the past, but the heart, breaking through the restrictions of reason, finds itself sufficient to the task.

THE RAISING OF LAZARUS

Chapter Five

THE MIRACLES OF JESUS

The Essenes of Syria and the Therapeutae of North Africa healed the sick with simple and natural remedies and also by exorcism and the reciting of verses from the Old Testament. Earlier, Pythagoras had treated disease by reading sections from the *Odyssey* of Homer. The Essenes had a secret book called *Sepher-rephori-oph*, which some said had been compiled by Solomon. Other sects of the region, including the Nazarites and the Ebionites, practiced the laying-on of hands and healing by prayer. This may account for the general lack of surprise or amazement over the miracles of Jesus. Even the Jewish priests attached to the Second Temple claimed the power to work miracles, and such wonders were comparatively regular occurrences. St. John, 7:13, according to the Codex Sinaiticus, causes the people to ask: "When Christ cometh will he do

107

more miracles than these which this man doeth?" The implication was that at this period of his ministry, Jesus had not been identified with the promised Messiah.

The descent of Christianity has been intimately associated with religious miracles. The power to produce such phenomena was not limited to the apostles, but has been associated with the lives of many pious theologians and mystics. Early church histories and the pseudohistorical accounts of saints and martyrs are resplendent with wonderful happenings. Even today, evidence by miracles is usually required for beatification or the canonization of a saint in the Roman Catholic Church, except in cases of martyrdom. In the course of centuries, miraculous power has come to be associated mostly with works of healing in the Christian communion. Since the Reformation, the Protestant descent of the faith has generally disregarded the older practice of healing the sick by divine grace, but occasionally it recurs in programs of evangelism.

The rising conflict between theology and science further reduced popular interest and public faith in the efficacy of spiritual therapy. Freedom of religious conviction has resulted in no conviction at all on this important subject. From the advent of the scientific method in the 17th century to the unfolding of the concept of psychology in the closing years of the 19th century, the miracle was considered little better than a pious fraud. Like many of the extreme attitudes which flourished in this era of intellectual skepticism, the prejudice against spiritual phenomena must be re-examined in the light of a larger knowledge.

There is nearly always some element of truth in a belief which has survived the vicissitudes of social and cultural change. Reports of miracles, sustained by the testimony of honorable witnesses, have descended from remote times and are to be found in all religious beliefs and on all levels of human development. It does not seem reasonable that such accounts are completely without substance. Even though imposture may have been practiced in some cases, this does not justify unqualified condemnation. If the miracle originates in a concept of divine intercession, the opponents of the doctrine can advance only their own concept that such intercession is impossible. The resultant controversy reveals prejudice, but does not increase knowledge.

Gibbon, in his *Decline and Fall of the Roman Empire*, writes: "The Christian Church, from the time of the Apostles and their disciples, has claimed an uninterrupted succession of miraculous powers, the gift of tongues, of visions and of prophecy, the power of expelling demons, of healing the sick and of raising the dead." It has been said that the miracles of Christ had doctrinal import and evidential value. As doctrine, they witnessed and sustained the ministry revealing the power of faith and the efficacy of prayer. Symbolically, these wondrous happenings shadowed prophetically the works of the spirit and the victory of the human soul over ignorance, sin, and death. As evidence, the miracles strengthened the devotion of the disciples and followers and were regarded by them as proof that the Master was divinely overshadowed.

The scientific concept of a universe ruled by immutable law made no provision for occurrences which seemed to conflict with, or be exceptional to, the regular processes of Nature. What appeared to be miraculous must have been an appearance rather than a fact. The Swiss physician and mystic, Paracelsus, defined a miracle as an effect, the cause of which was unknown, but which cause must inevitably be equal to the effect which it produces. By such reasoning, spiritual phenomena originate in the unexplored parts of the universe, which, being beyond human knowledge, cannot be estimated and which appear to be exceptional. Other types of incredible occurrences must be explained as delusions arising through faulty estimation of circumstances. Sincerity is quite possible, and the integrity of the witness is not challenged; it is the human judgment that is at fault.

A new dimension was bestowed by the researches of the pioneer psychologists. These demonstrated beyond reasonable doubt the power of the human mind over both body and environment. The internal life of the individual was accepted as the true cause of his external state. Psychoanalysis and psychotherapy lifted the causes of phenomena to the mental plane. The intensity of the mental-emotional focus was recognized as the proper cause of dispositional peculiarities otherwise inexplicable. This approach to the human mystery was bitterly opposed by the exponents of science on the one hand and the defenders of religion on the other hand. The situation remained comparatively unchanged until the introduction of the psychosomatic theory.

Through a series of clinical experiments, it has been demonstrated that the internal life of the individual profoundly influences his physical health. Negative or destructive thoughts and emotions disturb bodily function, causing various types of disorders, related symbolically to their causes. This discovery has led to a rapid advance in psychotherapeutic technique, especially in the field of therapy. The scientists, without realizing what they have done, have completely justified the Biblical statement: "As a man thinketh in his heart, so is he." Nor is it difficult in the light of this thinking to explain why "that which cometh out of the mouth defileth the man."

Although the causes of human distress are now attributed to the fallacies of the untutored mind, the term *mind*, as it is used by advanced psychologists, is taking on implications previously associated with the terms *soul* and *spirit*. By a long and difficult route, the modern intellectualist is returning to the essential convictions which dominated ancient thinking. He is proving the past and sustaining the doctrines dear to his ancestors, but he gives the old truths new names and thus escapes being stigmatized as a reactionary.

Psychosomatics advocates the sane mind in the sound body. It affirms this compound to be essential to the survival of normalcy. When we consider what constitutes actual sanity, we are immediately involved in philosophical speculations and mystical musings. A healthy internal life must be sustained by enduring values. Mental sickness is usually the result of a radical departure from hope, faith, and charity. The very abuses which religion has systematically opposed are responsible for many infirmities of the flesh. That which strengthens the soul in right purpose relieves the body from stress and tension. The Ten Commandments as given by Moses and the further commandments bestowed by Jesus and the recommendations contained in the Beatitudes are not only good for the soul, but also necessary to the health of the body. A kind, gentle, and tolerant religion inspiring dedication to right principles is as surely a system of therapy as any school of academic medicine. It would be conservative to say that at least half of all sickness is due to departure from the spirit of the golden rule. This is as surely a scientific fact as the law of gravity, and rather more vital.

Materialism has so reduced and restricted the application of the ethical and moral codes that human beings are sickened by their own conduct. Convinced that they cannot be true to themselves without being economically and socially penalized, otherwise honorable persons compromise their convictions, fully aware that they are sacrificing health and happiness. As rapidly as new medications are compounded for the treatment of recognized ailments, new ailments appear. We are still trying to treat the disorders of the internal life by poulticing, purging, and dosing the corporeal fabric. Even when the body is preserved, the soul remains sorely afflicted.

The phenomenal increase of religious interest in the past twenty years bears witness to an instinctive recognition of spiritual requirements. Harassed and frustrated mentally and emotionally, and disturbed physically by the consequences of these intensities, the individual is searching in his own way and according to his own ability for internal peace. Those who have been able to accomplish a measure of such tranquillity stand ready to testify to the beneficial results. Not only is living more meaningful and the simple and natural pleasures of life more enjoyable, but the body reveals a new vitality and a greater resistance to the corrosive influences of environment. Many sects have arisen devoted to what may be termed *religious therapy*. These groups sometimes hold extreme attitudes, but in the main they prove the validity of their claims. By giving a dynamic and persuasive impetus to constructive living and thinking, they have brought personality integration to thousands of their followers.

We are all inclined to justify our right to suffer. We have been grievously and sorely offended, and it seems perfectly natural to perpetuate a faithful account of the injustices which we have endured. We relive them daily, reveal them to our friends, and bestow them as a priceless heritage upon your descendants. We have been injured; why, then, should we not feel the pain? Tragedy has dogged our footsteps; is not this noteworthy? When we see others who appear more fortunate, is not this a just cause for melancholia or even a trace of resentment? Without realizing the processes involved, we are first injured and then injure ourselves. Both self-pity and self-censure create toxins which poison the difficulties of the heart and the mind. As this zone of infection enlarges, it pollutes the sources of our physical vitality, hastening the natural courses of disease and depressing function.

It is useless to evade the issue of living by justifying destructive habits and practices. We solve nothing in terms of body chemistry by proving that we have suffered or that another ill-starred mortal is to blame. We are punished, not by what is done to us, but by our reaction to the injury. To forgive our enemies and to bless those who despitefully use us are sound therapeutic measures. When a physician prescribes a certain regime for the patient, he does so because faulty habits are endangering health. Far more important than the habits of the body are the policies of the mind. The doctor may sense this and recommend that the sufferer relax, enjoy himself, cultivate new interests, and practice optimism. Unfortunately, those in greatest need of such advice are least able to apply it. Can we relax and enjoy ourselves merely by deciding to do so, but with no capacity for happiness? Can we be optimistic when as far as we are concerned everything is desperately wrong? No one can turn on and off long-established habits by a simple and direct action of the will. He may inhibit them for a time, but, like malignancies of the flesh, they will return unless the cause is corrected.

To be happier than we are requires that we should be better than we are and, perhaps at the moment better than we have any desire to be. The physician has an opportunity peculiar to his profession. Those who come to him are troubled, disturbed, and uncomfortable, and therefore most open to constructive suggestions. No one can endure suffering indefinitely without a growing determination to rid himself of the pain. If at this time he is told the facts, he is likely to be impressed. Even if the ailments are diagnosed as essentially physical, the organization of internal resources will contribute to a more rapid recovery and in extreme instances may determine survival.

When we are invited to take stock of ourselves, we often find that we are deficient in spiritual overtones. We have drifted along depending completely upon external conditions for happiness and peace of mind. Neither our educational advantages nor our practical experiences have enriched us as persons. Our associates are of our own kind, or they would not satisfy our inclinations. We have developed skill and judgment in order to insure financial survival, but we have made no provision for the day of personal adversity. We face life as we face death, with a melancholy hope.

Mysticism can be a wonderful help to those not inclined to seek consolation in congregational worship and sectarian confusion. We frequently hear people say that they have worked out a philosophy of living that meets their needs. This usually means that they have adjusted, in one way or another, to the prevailing temper and are doing the best they can in a difficult situation. Sustained by a few moral axioms partly practiced, they rest their case in the keeping of an understanding beyond their own. The dimensions of the concept are dim and the boundaries uncertain, but a little faith is certainly better than none.

The enrichment of character by the cultivation of positive convictions prepares the way for a larger appreciation of the universal mystery. Even though we see only in part, it requires but a slight extension of vision to sustain the basic elements of an enduring faith. In religion we grow by acceptance, but this does not mean that we are required to accept that which is essentially unreasonable. We have the right to acknowledge the existence of a Supreme Power of good, the immortality of the human soul, and the ultimate triumph of truth over error. Each of these acceptances has implications which can be unfolded and applied to the personal problems of living. We cannot believe that this universe is the product of infinite wisdom and infinite love and at the same time live in a state of rebellious disquietude. Each must struggle with his standard of values until light conquers darkness in his own heart.

It is not necessary to debate the merits or demerits of countless incidents. Once we have experienced a certainty of values, all the lesser doubts are thereby resolved. We apply a positive attitude, whereas previously we were content to react negatively. As misery feeds from its own substance, so hope nourishes itself. By reversing our own psychic impulse, we change the entire course of our thinking. Just as the mind of the maturing human being passes, by imperceptible stages, from the concerns of childhood to those of adulthood, the inner self experiences an increase of values. It is the intention of Nature that mankind shall grow, not only outwardly in terms of strength, but inwardly in terms of grace. Thus we fulfill destiny by self-improvement.

The miracles of Jesus, whether explained theologically or psychologically, testify to the power of spirit over material limitation. The man of soul brings with him the doctrine of tranquillity. Throughout the ministry the Master taught a wonderful program of mental and emotional hygiene. His own example of complete dedication to the divine will and obedience to the divine law are sure guides to health from within. Sickness came to mankind because human beings broke the law; and to free themselves from their infirmities, they must keep the law. We hear much from exponents of natural health methods about obeying Nature to insure the extension of physical efficiency. We also learn about the laws of the spirit and how we may obey them in order to preserve the integrity of the person in the body.

Beyond the simple requirements of daily function, the problem of health has a larger import. Judging from the length of the prenatal epoch and the period required for the human being to attain maturity, the life span of man should be from four to five times its present expectancy. Nature, which is the handmaiden of universal law, is a thrifty servant. She does not squander her resources, and is always and everywhere watchful and provident. The human body could certainly function longer and more efficiently if it were not afflicted by negative pressures both from within itself and from its environment. It is a well-established fact that longevity is promoted by simple living and gracious acceptance of the world's burden. It is not work but the friction caused by conflict that exhausts the vital resources. Worry, fear, hate, and inordinate ambition shorten life and condemn the closing years of human existence to decrepitude and misery.

We often insist that we could be happy and well-adjusted if others did not interfere with these worthy inclinations. Actually, no one has the power to destroy in another peace of mind, love of truth, or strength of faith. It is the lack of these very qualities or the incapacity to experience them that makes us vulnerable. We claim to have lost that which we never possessed. Once the life is dedicated to principle, we transmute by the alchemy of love any destructive thought or action that is turned against us. It is true that if our faith were equal to a mustard seed we could move a mountain, but remain immovable in our own conviction. The Greeks referred to the cathartic power of internal illumination. Even as light cleanses and purifies by its very presence, so love purges the heart and mind of their impurities. It is useless to say that the quality of our mercy has been strained or that our good resolutions have been overtaxed. Light is inexhaustible, and it is our own mind and not the God in our hearts that convinces us that we have endured too much. Ever on the defensive, we resent what we should accept and understand.

The cultivation of the mystical attitude first relieves us of our own neurotic tensions, and, by so doing, ends much environmental conflict. We must always remember that certain things happen to us because of ourselves. When a life falls into a pattern of recurrent misfortune, it is because the chemistry of the personality attracts such ills by a sympathetic power. We can change our lives by changing ourselves, but if we simply attempt to alter the outer pattern of our living without changing ourselves, the new pattern will soon be the same as the old one. There can be no release from conditions while as persons we remain in the same condition.

The first miracle of Jesus was the transforming of water into wine at the marriage feast in Cana. Water is the ancient symbol of purification, and wine, an equally old and venerated symbol of illumination. Thus the man of soul has the power to transform the water of baptism into the wine of ecstasy. The wedding feast was a most appropriate occasion, for it represented a union of lives, even as the mystical experience is often described as a spiritual marriage. The Master set the example for his disciples when he cleansed the lepers, opened the eyes of the blind, cast out demons, transformed substances, controlled the elements, healed the sick, raised the dead, and finally accomplished his own resurrection and witnessed it before the disciples. All these wonderful and strange happenings testify to the available power of God operating through one consecrated to the service of truth. Jesus instructed his disciples to continue in his name and to do the works which he had revealed. He empowered them with his own powers from God and sanctified them with his love. So, likewise, the Christ in you can sanctify, dedicate, and empower if the man of body will harken to the call: "Forsake your nets and follow me."

The faith content in human nature may, under certain intensities, miraculously increase. It is not possible for all to have faith in the same degree or of the same quality of integrity. Faith to one is a dynamic force; to another, merely a static acceptance. Sincerity and devotion determine, to a great measure, the availability of a sufficient faith. Shrines of healing have always testified to the benefits of devout belief. The Greeks and Egyptians had deities of medicine, and their sanctuaries were adorned with gifts of gratitude from those who came and were healed. Christianity has no divinities set apart for special services. Jesus was the teacher, the shepherd, and the physician. The Christian mystic unites his worship into one quality of devotion and seeks the fulfillment of all things needful through the act of prayer. In this, he recognizes one source of strength and one fountain of good. He sincerely believes, through an internal power of knowledge, that by the dedication of his soul to the service of the Christ power he is made new and whole in the spirit.

The miracle is not accomplished by the direct search for health, but by the experience of the inflow of the presence of God. We ask not that our aches and pains shall be taken from us, but that in our hearts we shall know that faith by which all perfect works are possible. There are many weaknesses, but only one strength. There are countless infirmities, but the fact of health is indivisible from the fact of truth. We cannot accomplish the lesser except through the greater. If we nourish the root of the tree, it will have many flowers and fruits, but if we attempt to perfect one of the fruits the tree may perish. The cause of health is identical with the cause of peace and security and one cannot be attained without the others.

To the mystic, the experience of internal revelation is itself miraculous. It transcends the expectancies of the mind and emotions, even as physical phenomena of an unusual nature transcend the expectancies of the objective faculties. The miracle, when separated from a sound religious doctrine, can lead to unfortunate results. The human being naturally seeks to escape from the restriction of law and order. He resents being required by divine power or human authority to practice a code of ethics which interferes with his more personal and selfish instincts. As an equation in living, the miraculous seems to offer a supernatural solution to situations, the full implications of which the mind wishes to evade. Why should we struggle so heroically for the improvement of character if the greater sinner can become the greater saint by mysterious means?

In this argument, our thinking is historical rather than personal. The miracle has not occurred to us, but is told of others about whom we have only reports and accounts. We are inclined to assume that which we desire to assume, and by this process we are led astray. Devotion to principles can be estimated in terms of extensity or intensity. Some may labor quietly over a considerable period of time, thus accomplishing a desired end. Others can accomplish similar objectives more rapidly by the intensification of soul power. In either case, cause and effect remain equal in quality, but this may not be evident to the physical sense perceptions. The mystical experience occurs on a certain plane of consciousness and is available to those who attain to this level. The interior circumstances of this attainment cannot always be estimated rationally; they must be known intuitively.

The departments of living in which we seem to stand in most immediate need of divine help are those in which our own abilities appear inadequate. These include obscure health problems, incompatibilities of temperament, and collective economic pressures. In these situations, we like to feel ourselves victims of forces or patterns beyond our control. We turn to prayer, seeking to avail ourselves of the spiritual resources of the universe. Only the miracle can accomplish that which is otherwise impossible or improbable. With our human limitations, we see no reason why we should not petition divine assistance to restore violated integrities. Unfortunately, we are not so much concerned with facts as we are with immediate requirements. Thus we have the phenomenon of two nations at war with each other, both praying to the same God for the victory of their causes.

When prayer is motivated by selfish or unenlightened impulses, it is more than likely that the granting of our petition would result in loss or hardship to others. To gain by another's loss and to accomplish at another's expense cannot be regarded as honorable or worthy. The misuse of spiritual power is sorcery, and those who engage in such action will ultimately suffer as a result. When we implore divine aid, it is nobler to ask that our own eyes be opened than that others should see the errors of their ways. The mystic solves the world enigma by releasing the light in his own soul and allowing this light to do the works of God by the miracle of love.

It has never seemed to me that we should require that the man of soul within us arbitrate the consequences of our human frailties. It is not God who should work for us, but we who should work for God. Soul in bondage to body is like the blinded Samson bound to the millstone of the Phillistines. We cannot deny the power of the spirit over phenomenal happenings, but we can question the integrity of using this power selfishly. The one necessary miracle is the redemption of ourselves by the power of grace. This redemption is not measured in the correction of circumstances, but in the strength of the enlightened self over circumstance.

Elevated by a simple and honorable faith to union with the substance of the divine love, the mystic requires no other consolation or evidence of the act of grace. He is born again, out of darkness into light, out of doubt into certainty. This participation in the very substance of sovereign reality re-orients completely the human perspective. The requirements of the man of soul are different from those of the man of body. What formerly appeared desirable or sufficient is no longer of paramount importance. Both the subject and object of prayer are internally altered. We know as a certainty of experience that what we give is more valuable than what we gain. We fulfill by releasing rather than by possessing, and find happiness in the well-being of others rather than in the advancement of ourselves. To seek the path of mysticism in order to accomplish worldly ends is either to fail or to come to that threshold of decision in which our selfish purposes are renounced and rejected.

Assuming for the moment that the mystical state has been attained, we find ourselves experiencing so complete an awareness of the rightness of things as they are and the certainty of the victory of good over evil that we are no longer inclined to ask or petition that things be changed. When we know as a certainty of the spirit that God is in his heavens and all is right with the world, we experience the repose of the soul. Many mystics have called themselves quietists, thus defining the subject of their quest. Quietude of the spirit and from the spirit is the peace of God. This gentle serenity transmutes confusion and discord at their sources and not after they have manifested their troubled works.

Devout faith inspires complete acceptance, and in this way accomplishes quietude. Action impelled by the consciousness of peace inevitably follows harmonious, rythmic, and orderly patterns. When only gentleness and beauty flow from within the person, there is, indeed, balm in Gilead. This balm is for the healing of both natures and nations. What more perfect solution can be found for the effects of tension than the ceasing of the tension itself? For example, tension manifests as intensity, and intensity is a pressure which impels to ill-considered activity. The more we act under the pressure of emergency, the more certainly we will act unwisely. This unwisdom, in turn, has consequences, and these take the forms of discord, conflict, and errors of judgment. As these negative factors increase within us and extend about us through their effects, we become tired, nervous, worried, and perplexed. Even if such negative attitudes do not immediately cause sickness, they will do so in time by impoverishing the vitality resources of the body.

If the majority of the peoples of the world are so afflicted from within themselves, we have the collective manifestations of these personal disquietudes. Racial and class hatreds and prejudices are intensified. Private irritations accumulate to become public animosities. The French criminologist, Bertillion, defined the criminal as a man who is sick. Individuals unhappy in themselves suffer from one of the most dangerous of all infectious and contagious diseases. Lack of spirit-anchorage in a sufficient faith is responsible for the unhappy social system which weighs so heavily upon its citizens. Can we not say that personal insecurity is a perpetual emergency requiring immediate consideration?

To the apostles, the greatest of all miracles of Jesus was his resurrection from the dead after three days in the tomb. Through this supreme manifestation of the power of God, the Master testified to the complete victory of spirit over matter. The mystic accepts the resurrection as the certain evidence of the victory of life within himself. As he follows in the footsteps of the Master, the pilgrimage does not end on Calvary, but on Mount Olivet. Faith must accomplish the final fulfillment of itself before its testimony is consummated. The universal life-principle is itself the source of processes more miraculous than the wonders associated with transcendental arts. We accept the miracles of Nature, but find it hard to estimate the miracles of religion. Actually, generation is as difficult to explain as regeneration. We accept the outward growth of creatures as they unfold the potentials locked in the seed, the egg, and the womb. Why, then, does it appear remarkable that faculties and propensities of the human compound should also enlarge and come to the fullness of their own potentials? If plants grow toward the light of the sun, why should not souls grow toward the light of God, which is the source of their nutrition? Growth is not miraculous, but the results of it as manifested to our sense perceptions appear wonderful and extraordinary. Physical evolution is revealed through a gradual improvement of species, and spiritual evolution by the gradual refinement of the qualities and attributes of man's internal disposition. Both processes are motions toward perfection, and perfection is fulfillment.

The miracles attributed to Jesus can be interpreted as testifying to growth. They were revelations of divine power moving from the invisible source of good through the human soul and into the mortal body or environment. Psychologists explain demonism as an obsession or possession of the mind by neurotic or psychotic areas of the subconscious. In simpler terms, we allow habitual attitudes to be so strengthened by repetition and revitalization that they finally gain control over the mind or emotions and possess us. Faith casts out demons by cleansing the consciousness of those destructive impulses which strengthen psychotic patterns. The dedication of the soul to works of light removes dangerous habits by a process of re-evaluation. What we cease to accept, we can no longer support.

Jesus cleansed the lepers as an evidence of his ministry. We are not certain from the reference in Leviticus, 13:14 that the disease so referred to was the same as that now recognized. It seemed to mean any serious sickness accompanied by progressive ulcerations on the surface of the body usually causing deformities and disturbances of sensation. Victims of such ailments were called unclean, and sentenced to a living death as social outcasts. Symbolically, those corrupted and diseased by their own vices and intemperances are the living dead. In the end, the internal wickedness corrupts the flesh and deforms the nature, destroying its sensitivity to all that is noble and beautiful. The ancients believed that disease was caused by sin, and the sovereign remedy was virtue.

Among the labors of Hercules was the cleansing of the stables of Augeias, which has the same meaning as the Greek myth of the solar deity. Light performs all the wonders, and light itself is but the outer form of life. The healing miracles may be interpreted mystically or literally. Here, again, the lesser is fulfilled by the greater, and that which is experienced in secret is revealed openly. The blessings which accompany the conversion of the soul to ways of truth are imparted to the body as the universal medicine described by the Hermetic philosophers. We are punished for wrongdoing by being imprisoned within the effects of our own actions. The corporeal part of man is the receptacle of consequences, and must bear witness to that by which it is contaminated.

It may not be agreeable to contemplate that our actions produce inevitable reactions, but we must accept the fact as a larger good than we choose to appreciate. Until we are resolved to correct causes, we have no right to be offended or displeased because of our afflictions. Illumination is a growth apart from time and is measured in the terms of dedication. We do not gain in virtue simply by enduring our infirmities with stoical composure. We are here to learn all lessons, but to accept only the fact of God's love.

The miracle of the raising of Lazarus has long been held to have special significance. Apparently the name is an abbreviated form of the old Hebrew *Eleazar*, which means *God's help*. Several persons of this name are mentioned in the Old Testament and include the third son of Aaron. This Eleazar later was invested with the sacred garments on Mount Hor, and succeeded Aaron in the office of high priest. The introduction of the name *Lazarus* into the parable of the beggar and the rich man (Luke, 16:19-31) is most curious. It seems to be related in some way to the story of Lazarus of Bethany, but the accounts conflict. It is also strange that so important a miracle as the raising of the brother of Martha and Mary after he had lain four days in the grave should be recorded only in the Gospel of St. John. The other Evangelists omit all mention of this wonderful occurrence. It has been suggested that St. John prepared his account after the other Evangelists had died. Possibly he waited until the persons involved had departed from this life and therefore could not be persecuted or embarrassed.

There is a mystical tradition that the raising of Lazarus described symbolically the establishment of a secret sect or school within the Christian communion. The religious mysteries of antiquity included in certain of their rituals a scene in which the candidates for initiation passed through a mystical death and resurrection. This ceremony implied a departure from worldliness and a rebirth in light and truth. The same thought is conveyed by the words of Jesus: "Except a man be born again, he cannot see the kingdom of God" (St. John, 3:30). In the sixth verse, the Master amplifies his original statement: "That which is born of the flesh is flesh; and that which is born of the Spirit is spirit." In Egypt and Greece, those mystics who had passed through the experience of the second birth were called the "twice-born" and were regarded with special veneration.

Birth into the physical world results in a limitation of internal consciousness. When the eyes of the body are open, the sight of the soul is obscured. Living unfolds on the plane of form until the person becomes so immersed in material concerns that he is unable to maintain the clarity of inner vision. By the mystical experience, he is released from the powers of mortality. He is reborn in the light and can know again the kingdom of heaven. Lazarus has come to be recognized as the embodiment of this process. The spirit in man does not die within the body, but sleeps until it is released by the experience of the mystical resurrection. It is known that Jesus instructed his disciples in many matters not revealed to the multitudes. Early Christian writers enlarged upon this theme, but without arriving at generally acceptable conclusions.

The miraculous draught of fishes is described in St. Luke, 5:2-9. This has been interpreted as foreshadowing the future power of the Christian ministry. Simon Peter was to become the great fisherman, the fisher of men. It was the work of the apostles to cast their nets into the sea of life and to draw forth food from the deep. The first symbol of the Christians was the fish, and during the persecutions in Rome they recognized each other by drawing the shape of a fish on the ground with their staffs. The miracle of supply, with its over-tones and implications, certainly referred to the food of the spirit. Those who have perfect faith say in their hearts, with Simon: "At thy word I will let down the net." There is ample evidence that those who accept the way of the inner life are wonderfully preserved and protected by their own integrity.

In practical daily living, we often labor long and sincerely, yet the ends we seek are not accomplished. We struggle on, becoming more desperate and troubled as our efforts fail. At last, discouraged, we abandon the project, only to find that as we renounce the intention it is fulfilled. Experience teaches us that we lose much by trying too hard and by allowing personal pressures and intensities to interfere with the natural workings of divine law. Before the good things we seek can come to us, we must increase in love, wisdom, peace and faith. The goodness in our hearts draws to us that which is needful. We must become more thoughtful about our inner lives if we would attain honorable success in our temporal careers. Here, again, the greater miracle is the power of the spirit.

The opening of the eyes of the blind is an obvious allusion to spiritual apperception. There are none so blind as those who will not see. The sight of the eyes is perfected by the light in the heart and mind. Those who see only the outer forms of things and have no vision of the life processes within and behind bodies have failed to use properly the faculties with which they have been endowed.

We never see clearly until sight supports understanding and the interior faculties transmute the findings and reports of the exterior perceptions. While it may be true that the physical eyes can not behold the universal mystery, they do make available substantial evidence of the workings of God. This evidence, when honestly and faithfully reported to a mind gently receptive to spiritual values, strengthens faith, deepens understanding, and inspires courage and dedication. When the man of soul within us becomes the master of our purposes, we instinctively observe and comprehend that which is concealed from those less enlightened. When we ask a man if he understands us, we may say to him: "Do you see the meaning?" We imply sight by the reason or by the emotional attributes of consciousness. Thus, to see is really to comprehend, to recognize, or to know the essential substance of ideas.

In Matthew, 17:24-27 is described the miracle of the coin in the fish's mouth. At Capernium, those who collected tribute money came to Peter asking if Jesus paid tribute. The Master then told the disciple to go to the sea, cast the hook, and he would find a piece of money in the mouth of the first fish that was taken. This money was then to be given as tribute. This is one of the several instances in which Jesus set the example of rendering unto Caesar that which was Caesar's. Mystics have interpreted these actions as admonitions to obey the established laws of nations and times. Religion does not justify or require that the believer should set an example which may contribute to the delinquencies of others.

Internal growth does not confer freedom from law, but freedom within law. The Master taught that the progress of human institutions is not achieved by overthrowing the past, but by outgrowing the past. Faith is not violent, but it is inevitable in its workings. It changes all things, but does not burden society with revolutions and insurrections. As we improve, we naturally turn away from the lesser and embrace the greater. We often do this by a simple and gentle act of interpretation. We find new and richer meanings for old customs and procedures, and by living these new meanings we redeem the laws as we perfect ourselves. The fish was the symbol of spiritual supply, and later became the peculiar monogram of Christ. It lived in the ocean or sea of God, the depths of which no man has explored. The creature which inhabited water lived in the element of purification. The coin in its mouth was the abundance which is available from the spirit. This abundance takes any necessary form. When tribute is demanded, it is available if the inner life is established in godliness.

Matthew, 12:10-13 combines a miracle with a traditional observance. A man with a withered hand came to Jesus on the Sabbath to be healed. The Pharisees asked the Master if it was lawful to perform the act of healing upon the Sabbath day. Jesus answered by questioning them, concluding that it was lawful to do a good deed on any day. He then healed the withered hand, and departed because the Pharisees held council against him. In ancient religions, the hand was regarded as the instrument of the will and the purpose. That which is conceived in the mind or the heart is manifested through the works of the hand. Ultimately, the hand became the symbol of civilization itself, which is the monument to the labor and industry of mankind. The withered hand, like the barren tree, fails of usefulness. The man of soul extends his power to his parts and members, dedicating them to his service. We remember the words: "If I forget, O Jerusalem, let my right hand forget *her cunning.*" If we fail truth, our right hand has already lost its cunning, but its skill is restored if we restore truth in our own hearts.

Boehme applied the term Sabbath to the great peace in the soul of one who has experienced the mystical Christ. In six days we labor, and by this labor is meant the works of growth. We struggle through the mystical equivalent of the six creative processes. All profitable labor is growth toward truth by the unfoldment of character. If we have worked well and have been good and faithful servants through the College of the Six Days Work, we come on the seventh day to the peace of God. We rest in the spirit, not because we seek idleness or leisure, but because in quietude we are called to a larger endeavor. The mystical experience is the Sabbath in which we set aside the time of God.

All the miracles are included in the feeding of the multitude. Jesus divided five loaves of bread and two fishes, feeding more than five thousand persons and having left thereafter twelve baskets full of fragments (Matthew, 14:15-21). The bread is the food of the earth, and the fishes the spiritual nutrition from the sea of space. Here is the promise that the experience of truth shall, indeed, be the source of infinite supply. All the miracles of the spirit are works of supply. From within ourselves come the healing, nourishing, protecting, and providing power. When we know this with a complete and sufficient faith, we are established in righteousness.

MYSTERY OF SPIRITUAL ALCHEMY

Chapter Six
THE LORD'S PRAYER

A prayer is a formula of supplication, adoration, confession, or thanksgiving addressed to God, either directly or through intermediary powers by an individual or a congregation. The words may be fixed by traditional usage or may be completely informal according to the mood or need of the supplicant. In either case the words themselves must be spoken with the deepest sincerity and the fullest realization of the sacredness of the petition. Prayers of ancient nations are recorded upon surviving monuments, especially those pertaining to mortuary rites or public offerings in honor of remarkable events. Such prayers are similar to those in use today, and there has been very little change in the structure of prayer-formulas since the earliest recorded examples.

Since the Protestant Reformation, the practice of private prayer has increased among Christian nations. The ritualistic forms of the older churches have been modified, and prayer has become an intimate experience of faith. Although some churches have maintained the form of congregational petition, the individual members of the church are encouraged to seek spiritual security, especially in times of stress, through the act of private prayer. Form and words are regarded as less important than the genuine statement of faith made either audibly or silently, and it is assumed that Deity, mindful of the needs of his children, will be attentive to all honorable and honest petitions. It is well known that philosophers and scholars, not given to the acceptance of most theological forms, have practiced the act of prayer and recommended it to their students and disciples.

The transition between prayer as a ritual and prayer as a mystical experience has been accomplished gradually through the increasing emphasis upon religion as a personal search for truth. As the result of the mingling of traditions with the instincts of the human soul, the impulse to seek solace in prayer is widespread even among those not nominally religious. This is clearly revealed in times of public disaster, war, and other general catastrophes. The human being is most aware of his own limitations when his character is subjected to unusual pressures. When insufficient to his own needs, he is impelled to seek a larger source of security. It requires but slight consideration on his part to realize that faith has brought courage and consolation to other persons whom he has known, admired, or loved. Early religious indoctrination and association intensify the resolution, and the mind easily accepts such persuasions. There are very few who choose to walk dark and dangerous paths alone, and as the way becomes more hazardous, the benefits of spiritual communion become more evident.

Few modern religious institutions have escaped materialistic pressures, and the churches are confronted with decisions which require genuine dedication to truth. The act of prayer is too often involved in the gratification of personal and physical ambitions. The believer prays more for prosperity in this world than for security in the world to come. He is more concerned with the increase of his goods than with the increase of the power of good within himself. Instead of approaching Divinity with humility and thankfulness, the prevailing tendency is to bombard heaven with requirements and demands. In many cases we ask for that which we have neither the resolution nor the patience to earn by legitimate means. To the degree that prayer becomes a substitute for common intelligence and natural industry, the mood of prayerfulness is mutilated and profaned.

Religious supplication is usually a petition for something lacking and needful or a request that something present and harmful be removed. When the difficulty should be corrected or the lack supplied by the individual himself, it is his ethical responsibility to apply such remedies as are within his knowledge before asking for divine help. Religion, as a guide to character and conduct when properly and faithfully practiced, will reduce the emergencies which impel man to ask for higher assistance. When one of his disciples questioned Pythagoras concerning the advisability of supplicating the gods, the great sage recommended that only the wisest of men should ask favors of the deities.

He explained that only those who had outgrown personal ambition and prejudice would be likely to pray for the good of others. Pythagoras explained that most men will pray for what they want, but only the gods understand the human need. If an unwise prayer be granted, disasters are only multiplied.

The prayer generally known as the Lord's Prayer is used throughout Christendom and is treasured by most, if not all, of the Christian sects. Although it is generally supposed that the words were revealed by Jesus for the use of his disciples and followers, it was actually derived from older Jewish prayers, and contains nothing that is inconsistent with the Rabbinical tradition. Basnage (see *His. des Juifs*, t. VI. p. 374) has said that the Jews had an ancient prayer, called the Kadish, exactly like the Lord's Prayer, and Webster may well remark that it is a curious fact that the Lord's Prayer may be constructed almost verbatim out of the Talmud.

The anonymous author of that most learned work, *On Mankind, Their Origin and Destiny* (London, 1872), reprints from Reverend John Gregorie (London, 1685) the following Jewish prayer: "*Our Father which art in heaven*, be gracious to us, O Lord our God; *hallowed be thy name*, and let the remembrance of thee be glorified *in heaven* above, *and upon earth* here below. Let *thy kingdom* reign over us, now and forever. Thy holy men of old said, Remit and *forgive* unto all men whatsoever they have done against me. *And lead us not into temptation, but deliver us from* the *evil* thing. *For thine is the kingdom*, and thou shalt reign in *glory, for ever* and for evermore." Those parts not in italics are omitted in the Christian version.

It is not necessary here to examine parallel references in Hebrew writings to the various elements of the Lord's Prayer. "Our Father which art in heaven" occurs repeatedly in Jewish compositions prior to the Christian Era. The expression "give us this day our daily bread" is in the Talmud, attributed to Hillel. We may say, therefore, that a number of early convictions and expressions of veneration and worship have been combined into a simple and devout prayer. The very arrangement suggests that the form may have been influenced by the mystical sect of the Essenes.

The stream of early Christian mysticism followed a circuitous course in its descent through the centuries. It absorbed into itself a diversity of religious and philosophical teachings which supported its primary tenet— the fact of faith. The internal search for spiritual security was only possible in a universe so constructed and so governed that union with the Sovereign Good was predestined and foreordained. Illumination is the conscious apperception not only of the truth of good, but also of the vast machinery by which good is known to be a fact. Thus faith is demonstrable to those who have shared in its substance. Mystics have not only received into their hearts the love of God, but have beheld, in their raptures, the magnificent spectacle of a world growing and unfolding in and through the divine wisdom.

All religions affirm the reality of God-consciousness. The perfect wisdom, love, and power of the eternal Father brought forth the creation, which in its every part reveals the perfection of its source. As human hearts and minds open and receive into themselves the testimonies of the divine sovereignty, admiration becomes adoration. Faith leads inevitably to identity with the object itself. In Colossians, I:16, Paul the apostle writes

of God: "For by him were all things created, that are
in heaven, and that are in earth, visible and invisible,
whether they be thrones, or dominions, or principalities,
or powers: all things were created by him and for him..."

Those creations which are invisible, together with
their thrones and dominions, have received slight attention from modern religionists. That which lies beyond the objective sense-perception is of little concern
while we live in this material sphere. We ask the help
of heaven without any concept of how this assistance is
to be given. When a loved one departs from us, we may
affirm that he has gone to a better place. Jesus told his
disciples that in his Father's house were many mansions,
but we have not been impelled to inquire about these
abodes. We think of heaven as a blessed land beyond
the grave, and our definitions seldom influence the
skeptical. Assuming that the invisible is unknowable,
we devote our serious endeavors to the improvement of
physical living.

The words of those seers and saints who have
brought us tidings of great joy about the universe that
lies beyond the veil of matter are usually ignored. Even
if we believe or desire to believe, we are preoccupied
with worldliness. The spiritual unfoldment of humanity
requires the strengthening of those faculties of the soul
by which we must explore the hidden side of life's
threshold. These are the faculties which make possible
the mystical experience. Only those who cultivate the
spiritual instruments now latent within the heart and
mind can know the truth. This is the burden of The
Revelation of St. John, which describes symbolically
what happens to a seer when he passes through the
little door in the wall of heaven.

The power of prayer is released through the personal acceptance of the fact of God. The quality of the petition reveals the level of our own integrity and the degree of our own devotion. We cannot sincerely ask for help unless we believe that it is available, nor can we wisely and lovingly require that which is harmful to others. If faith is strong and deep, we cannot ask God to be merciful, for we know that mercy is a natural attribute of Deity. In the same spirit, it is unreasonable to beseech God to be mindful, patient, forgiving, or gentle. Such a request implies that we doubt the very divinity of Deity. It is our right and privilege to seek through prayer that which is not within our power to know or to accomplish through our own endeavors. The more perfectly we apperceive the wonders of the divine plan, the less likely we are to doubt the immediate availability of spiritual strength.

As one Christian mystic so well said, there is no need to ask for light; rather we should pray that our own sight shall be clear so that we may behold the light which is forever here. By this attitude our petition is one of acceptance and glorifies truth, even while we lack the inner wisdom to experience it fully. As the mystic grows in grace, prayer becomes a testimony of gratitude and a restatement of dedication to the divine plan. Instead of asking for what we want, we give thanks for what we have. We all live in a world of infinite opportunity surrounded by infinite goodness. As we come to realize this, all personal emotions are dissolved in gratitude. This was the spirit of old prayer; it was a song from the heart, a song of joy, and not a dirge of mortal woe. Faith transforms the ideals of man even as it reforms his appetites and instincts. Those of little faith require endless proof and demonstration; those of larger faith are filled with thankfulness.

Prayer creates a mystical mood—a strange, calm atmosphere blessing the inner life. This mood rewards itself and bestows its own benediction. There is no virtue in prayer unless it is accompanied by internal peace. It is this peace which is the proof of the covenant between heaven and earth. The peace that comes from faith is the perfect prayer because it is the complete tribute. We have accepted the divine will and the divine way, and from this perfect acceptance we have experienced the perfect consolation. Even though the words be faulty or we find it impossible to express the love and beauty that we feel, our love is the silent tribute of our intention.

In prayer we depart a little way from exterior concerns and abide in an atmosphere of sanctity. On such occasions we pierce the veil which divides our mortal condition from our eternal state. We receive nutrition from the spirit, and this food sustains the nobler impulses of our character. This is the food of silence—the bread of peace and the waters of everlastingness. As our bodies are fed from the earth, our souls are nourished by heaven. When we have partaken of this wonderful food, we shall not hunger again. As manna fell from the sky to feed the children of Israel, so the life of God flows into human hearts and minds nourishing them. Through prayer, then, we approach the source of life and partake of the bread of righteousness.

The act of prayer involves a series of personal acceptances. We acknowledge the power of God, we affirm the presence of this power, and we accept a concept of life which teaches the supreme importance of personal sanctity. Not only do we intuitively experience these values, but silently or audibly we state them in appropriate words. Statement itself integrates conviction, and through it we further clarify the dimensions of our own belief. The act of worship constitutes a formal declaration of faith, and prayer is a simple and direct religious action. The rite cannot be substituted for the fact, but it can, and does, bear witness to that which is in essence formless and beyond definition. Thus prayer clarifies the internal process of visualization. We see, in the sense of knowing, with a greater degree of intensity when we declare that which we affirm to be true.

Prayer has always been closely associated with mysticism as a natural and gentle method of releasing consciousness from the pressures of worldliness. For many persons it is the only available way of liberation from the burdens of objectivity. In this secret communion we express ideals and convictions otherwise locked within us. Those who pray together have known an association not to be found in other relationships. We can pray for the common good when all other forms of public service seem impossible. In so doing, we also perpetuate constructive instincts of our own.

Even those psychiatrists who are opposed to religious beliefs regretfully admit the value of prayer as a corrective mechanism. Very few psychotics past the age of forty-five years respond to psychotherapy unless they have faith in a divine power. If religious fanaticism is a menace to mental and physical health, atheism, which may also be fanatical, is equally detrimental. Both extremes represent pressures, and all pressure results in distress. It is not the principle of religion but the abuse of the human impulse to venerate which transforms the rite of prayer into an escape mechanism.

The prayers of various nations reveal the moral and ethical levels of these peoples, and the same is true of individuals. When we ask for a modification of the divine will, we assume that we possess the wisdom and insight which would justify our petition. The stronger our egotism, the more we demand; the less we understand, the more certain we are that we are being mistreated or misunderstood. The quality of our requests is also revealing. Most prayers are essentially selfish, not because we so intend, but because we are so constituted. Living intensely personal lives and reacting personally to every occurrence, it is only natural that we should invoke the aid of heaven to advance our cherished projects. There can be no true mystical content or spiritual comfort while motives are largely ulterior. If religion becomes only a metaphysical means of attaining physical ends, we defeat our search for a better way of life.

In St. Luke, 11:1-13, Jesus explained prayer to his followers. One of the disciples said to him: "Lord, teach us to pray, as John also taught his disciples." After reciting for them what is now called the Lord's Prayer, Jesus spoke thus: "If a son shall ask bread of any of you that is a father, will he give him a stone? or if he ask a fish, will he for a fish give him a serpent? Or if he shall ask an egg, will he offer him a scorpion? If ye then, being evil, know how to give good gifts unto your children: how much more shall your heavenly Father give the Holy Spirit to them that ask him?"

It should be specially noticed that Jesus said that the gift which the Father bestows upon those who earnestly petition is the Holy Spirit. This is the Comforter, and the reward for prayer is consolation and not worldly goods. The Lord's Prayer has richer meaning for us if we interpret it mystically and not literally. The purpose of religion is to enrich the spiritual graces and powers of the soul, and it is the presence of the Comforter which makes possible the victory of faith over worldliness. The bread of this world we earn by our labor, but the bread of heaven we earn by our love.

Mystics, scholars, and philosophers have given deep and wonderful explanations and interpretations of the Lord's Prayer. There are at least seven keys to the wording, but on this occasion we are concerned only with the devotional meaning. For this reason also there is no need to examine the wording according to the old languages or to debate the suitability of the prevailing translations. The beautiful prayer is part of the spiritual heritage of Christendom and its gentle words have been accepted by millions of devout persons without question or reservation. To change these lines, to correct them or to improve them would be an offense to many. After all, it is the spirit and not the letter which brings the Comforter.

Jesus taught: " . . . therefore pray ye: Our Father which art in heaven, Hallowed be thy name." (Matt. 6:9). This is the experience of God as the divine parent. We share in the realization that we are all the children of the eternal light. Our relation to our own source is reverent but not servile. A son does not humiliate himself to honor his father, nor does he regard himself as hopelessly in debt to his parents. Even fathers and mothers must earn and hold by their own conduct the natural admiration of their children. It was according to the divine plan that God brought forth the creatures to make plentiful his creation, with a wisdom and love beyond mortal understanding. The heavenly Father serves and protects his progeny. If we truly love him we keep his laws and serve one another in his name and through his powers within us. We have the right and privilege to remember the Creator in the days of our youth, and in the fullness of our years. We honor God most by acknowledging his plan through an appropriate code of conduct.

The word *heaven,* as it is used in religious writings, has slight semantic definition. In old scientific books, it meant that quality of space which contained the sidereal bodies. As a place, heaven was infinitely remote from the earth, a hypothetical sphere which enclosed the universe. Theology defined heaven as either a place or a state which was the abode of God and divine beings. It contained a part set aside as the ultimate home of perfected or redeemed human souls. Ancient philosophers defined heaven as the world of causes, the first and original source of life, and a receptacle into which all living things finally return. Such explanations are all more or less intellectual approaches to an unknown quantity or quality.

In mysticism, heaven is experienced as a condition of union with the divine nature. It is a spiritual atmosphere which can be known by the soul after dedication to truth. The Christian mystic becomes aware of heavenliness as a state of perfect internal faith and peace, an infinite well-being and security more real than any earthly environment. Heaven is within us and about us and can be discovered by the simple act of devotion. The mystical experience elevates the consciousness into a realm of infinite bliss where all good things are undeniable certainties. In a way, heaven is divine certainty, even as earth is mortal uncertainty. The Father in heaven is the divine power residing in the divine state.

To find peace in the love of God is to abide in the state of heavenliness.

Hallowed is a word of Anglo-Saxon origin meaning *made holy, blessed,* or *consecrated.* There is the subtle implication that it is the worshiper who must sanctify the object of his adoration. God is known to be blessed by an extension of human understanding. We become aware of holiness as our own souls accept the internal evidence of the eternal good. Needless to say, we can truly honor only that which we understand. It is the growth of ourselves which makes possible the apperception of divinity. As we increase in light, we become aware of the wonders of the light. This awareness is our direct way of blessing or making holy the invisible cause of our existence. Thus we consecrate our faith by consecrating ourselves in that faith.

The name of God is not any one or more of the seventy-two titles or designations which have been bestowed upon Deity by the religions of mankind. In mysticism, the true name can be spoken only by those who have experienced the substance of Divinity. All other titles or appellations are merely symbolical descriptions of attributes, qualities, or powers. God means *the good,* but only those who have known the atmosphere of the good within their own hearts can discover the secret of the name. Adam named the creatures of the field according to their forms and appearances. Those internally illumined bestow new names honoring the souls of living things. We can only honor that which we have known inwardly. What we are satisfied to name, we will never know, and what we have known no longer requires to be named. The name of God is therefore the complete substance of God known in a mystery of consciousness.

Having substantiated our faith by acknowledging ourselves receptive to its substance, we continue the prayer: "Thy kingdom come. Thy will be done, in earth as it is in heaven." Two complete concepts are contained in this section. Early worshipers were convinced that at a certain time the kingdom of heaven would be established upon the earth; the heavens would open, and the glory of the Lord, surrounded by angels, would be revealed to all men. Christ would come to restore the kingdom which had been lost through the fall of Adam. The triumphant army of the light would war against darkness and overcome the hosts of evil. That was the day of judgment, and those who had kept the faith would be united forever in a state of blessedness. Actually, the prayer does not contain this promise; rather it is a statement of conviction referring to an eternal fact.

The peace of God known by mystical communion is the coming of the kingdom. The worshiper is actually saying: "Let thy kingdom come in me." This is why the expected millennium has always been postponed as a historical or political occurrence. Man can receive into his own soul the growing awareness of the presence of God. As he becomes receptive to the mystery, he is filled with it. When the kingdom enters into him, he enters into the kingdom. Outward things do not seem to be changed, but they are made new by the spirit. When a sufficient number of dedicated persons have accepted the works of the spirit, the outer form of human cultural institutions and political systems will seem to grow and be perfected. St. Luke, 17:20, 21 clarifies the teachings of Jesus on this point: "And when he was demanded of the Pharisees, when the kingdom of God should come, he answered them and said, The kingdom of God cometh not with observation: Neither shall they say, Lo here! or, lo there! for, behold, the kingdom of God is within you." There is an alternative reading for the words *within you*, which can also mean *among you*.

The second statement of faith expands the first injunction: Let the will of God be done in earth as it is manifested in heaven. The will-aspect of Divinity is revealed through the laws by which the world was created, is maintained, and shall ultimately fulfill the divine purpose. All men naturally desire to know in order that they may co-operate consciously and serve with understanding. The revelation of the divine purpose was restated by Jesus when he went to pray on the Mount of Olives: "Father, if thou be willing, remove this cup from me: nevertheless not my will, but thine, be done." (St. Luke, 22:42) Human resistance to the will of God and mortal disobedience to the law of God are responsible for most of the disasters which have plagued humanity. Order is brought forth out of chaos, and peace is possible in this world only when we permit heaven to fulfill its ways upon the earth. The humility of mysticism is not resignation but acceptance. It is conscious at-one-ment, which is the only real atonement. We atone for disobedience, not by repentance and sorrow, but by obeying.

In the world of causes, which is heaven, the great principles of life manifest themselves in their natural state. In the sphere of effects, which we call the earth, the divine powers are obscured by the veil of matter and are so immersed in forms and bodies that we are unaware of their intentions. While we exist in corporeal limitation, we must seek with all our strength and devotion the evidences of the will of God. Part we discover through observing Nature; part by examining the characters of ourselves and others; and part through the internal faculties of the soul. Once we have learned, we are required by knowledge itself to conduct ourselves according to that knowledge. The kingdom of heaven comes to the material world when those living in this dark sphere walk in the light which they have discovered in their own hearts.

The prayer continues: "Give us this day our daily bread. And forgive us our debts, as we forgive our debtors." The mystic becomes so completely aware of the omnipresence of God that he cannot divide one kind of benefit from another. He is grateful for the gentle and loving presence that is always with him, making his way straight, and comforting him in his misfortunes. The more he puts his faith in God, the more aware he becomes of divine supply and protection. He can therefore give thanks for all the blessings that he receives and shares. Bread, which is the nutrition of his body and the staff of his physical life, becomes symbolic of all the good things that have been added by faith. There is a deeper meaning, however, for this bread is the complete nutrition which feeds both the inner and outer bodies. The inner body is the soul, which is the real self, the person concealed within the shell of form. Plato said that the body is the sepulcher of the soul, and in another writing he explained that the soul is contained within the body as the oyster is contained within the shell.

There is a Greek fable about the banquet of the sages. The wise assembled around a festive board to feed their hearts and minds. The food that they ate was music and poetry, and they discoursed together about divine mysteries and the wonderful works of wisdom.

Then each, refreshed and strengthened, departed to his own house to continue the activities to which he was accustomed. How seldom in these days do we share together the food of the spirit. We are content to nourish the body and to ignore the natural hunger of the soul which longs for beauty, faith, and love. As grain grows upon the earth and is made into bread, so the goodness of God which descends from heaven becomes the bread of the wise. They eat not for themselves only, but break this bread, which is the body of a blessed God, and share it with all who hunger. As we must earn our physical food by labor, so we must also perform those works by which we are entitled to our share of the eternal food. The symbolism is so simple that we have misunderstood its meaning. We are the ones who, asking for bread, are content to give ourselves the stone. In the mystical sacraments, Christ is the bread which came down from heaven to feed those who hungered and thirsted after righteousness. The Christ in us is the bread of life in our own souls.

The forgiveness of sin appears unreasonable unless it is explained in terms of mysticism. In a universe governed by love and wisdom, it is hard to accept the existence of sin. Perhaps the word actually means *to fall short, to be insufficient* or *imperfect* rather than *evil.* Learned commentators have so interpreted it, and with the authority of sincere convictions. It is obvious that imperfection is natural to all creatures existing in this mortal world. It is lack of sufficiency which impels us to the eternal quest for spiritual security. The debts for which we ask forgiveness are the consequences of our own mistakes. We plead to be understood, our frailties to be considered, and our limitations to be accepted. The spirit is willing, but the flesh is weak, and when we would do good, selfishness is always near. It is easy to be sentimental about our own imperfections and to justify our own imperfect works. The mystic accepts the obvious facts without question, and applies to others the same forbearance which he asks heaven to exercise on his behalf.

The proof that we recognize our own weaknesses is that we are also able to accept the shortcomings of our associates. We have no right to excuse our faults and then condemn others for the same mistakes. Mysticism removes the conviction of judgment from the human mind. We no longer have any desire to judge or to force our preconceptions upon others. We seek the experience of the discovery of God in the neighbor, the friend, the stranger, and even the enemy. We can never have peace in our own hearts while we resent the actions of those around us. In revenging ourselves upon them, we destroy our own security. Lives devoted to resentment and criticism and condemnation are wasted. We do a greater harm to our own natures than to the person who is the object of our animosity. He cannot be injured by us, nor can he be punished by us, but we can injure and punish ourselves trying to hurt him.

The same is true of those who do not actively practice the code of an eye for an eye and a tooth for a tooth. Some, believing themselves to be the victims of injustice, are content to grieve and to retire into an inner world of self-pity and forlorn memories. These assume, because they are not militantly avenging themselves, that they are good and honorable citizens of God's universe. We have no more right to injure the spirit of good within ourselves than we have to afflict our neighbor. The heart and mind burdened with a sense of injustice, profanes the living sanctuary of the soul. The inner life must be kept in holiness, full of good thoughts and gentle reflections. One of the reasons why so few attain the consolation of the spirit is that they are too conscious of their own troubles. In a wonderful universe divinely governed, they are the miserable victims of injustice. For such as these, the experience of the presence of God is not possible, they are too full of their own conceits.

If we forgive ourselves for what we have done to others, and we do this by a subtle process of personal exoneration, we must go further. Have we really been the victims of ingratitude, jealousy, and conspiracy? To what degree can another person injure us if our own souls are established in righteousness? Can the Divine within us be so easily offended, displeased, and disquieted? Is it not more likely that we are suffering from our own mistakes and shortcomings while shifting the blame to other unfortunate mortals? Happiness and peace come from the spirit and are not the result of the actions of our acquaintances. If each man must find peace for himself by deserving a better life, does it not follow that the unrest and discontent which disturb us come also from within and bear witness to the lack of honest faith and unselfish love? The very concept of forgiveness is reform, and all that we can do is to state through prayer that we know the truth and that through this knowledge we shall attain freedom. We cannot change others, but we can change ourselves; therefore, the plan of our redemption does not require that which is beyond our means. By changing ourselves, we experience a new sense of values, and our attitudes toward others are refined. As our own hearts are enriched, we discover new virtues and beauties in those whom we previously disliked.

The proper standard of human conduct is clearly stated by Jesus in Matt. 6:14, 15: "For if ye forgive men their trespasses, your heavenly Father will also forgive you: But if ye forgive not men their trespasses, neither will your Father forgive your trespasses." As we look about us and realize how few persons are naturally inclined to overlook the shortcomings of others and how eagerly they perpetuate their grievances, we can more easily understand why human relationships are discordant. Each generation seems less patient, less tolerant, and less willing to adjust to common needs. We would all be happier if the god-fearing were more humanity-loving. When we forgive through larger understanding, we overcome corrosive processes which are destroying ourselves. No one is really better or happier because he criticizes or condemns. Negative attitudes, if permitted to continue uncorrected, transform the personality from a noble compound into a disagreeable complex of tensions and neuroses.

When we cease disliking, we liberate ourselves from a negative psychic chemistry. The reform rewards itself. We become more attractive, which means that we are able to attract to ourselves more of the universal good. The mystic, by regarding all life as essentially sacred and noble, lives in a world of beauty which he has discovered by the adventure of growth. If we have faith in our hearts, it is easier to see good than evil. The eye of the soul is single because the purpose of the soul is undivided. This mystery is explained by the Master in Matt. 6:22, 23: "The light of the body is the eye: if therefore thine eye be single, thy whole body shall be full of light. But if thine eye be evil, thy whole body shall be full of darkness. If therefore the light that is in thee be darkness, how great *is* that darkness!"

The eye that is evil is that faculty which sees or discovers evil. If wherever we go we are aware first of faults and shortcomings and accept these as the facts, our lives are full of darkness and we deny the glory of our Maker. It is easy to develop the habit of suspicion. It gratifies us to assume that others are less perfect than ourselves. We attempt to sustain the dignity of our own characters by depreciating the dispositions of our associates. Unfortunately, when we are ever ready to see evil, we gradually come to believe in the reality of evil. In the end, we doubt all things, including the benevolence of God. From this doubt comes fear, which, in turn, destroys the good hope.

To a degree at least, this explains the next section of the prayer: "And lead us not into temptation, but deliver us from evil." As a noun, the word *evil* means *anything impairing happiness or welfare,* or *depriving of good.* In mysticism, an evil person is one whose divine nature is unable to manifest its purposes. This part of the prayer has been the cause of considerable controversy. It does not seem consistent that we should petition the divine source of love and wisdom by asking that it shall not lead us into temptation. Yet, in this same world fashioned and sustained by God, temptation is a fact. We are constantly invited to compromise our principles and to engage in selfish and destructive activities. Temptation results from human interpretation of the will of heaven. Even as we enlarge in wisdom, we increase in skillfulness. Skill in itself is not moral; it is simply the ability to accomplish certain desired ends. Human wisdom and mortal love can be so perverted as to destroy that which they most cherish. It is not easy to refrain from excess, and even the highest of our impulses can be corrupted if enthusiasm becomes fanaticism. Contemplation of God and of the wonders of his universe can result in a kind of spiritual pride personified as the fallen angel.

That which most completely inhibits and impairs the perfect expression of the divine will is ignorance. In this way, ignorance is the greater evil. To be delivered from evil is to be brought out of the darkness of unknowing. We go to school to learn the ways of human society and to fit ourselves for useful careers. The mystic must also go to school, and one described himself as a young pupil in the School of the Holy Spirit. We are not born into the mortal world so endowed that we may fulfill its requirements without proper discipline. The musician may be filled with harmonies and melodies, but he must train his body if he would bestow his gift upon the world. We cannot pass from the outer life of our kind to the inner life of mysticism without preparing ourselves for this experience.

Gradually, through the practice of the principles of the spiritual life, we become learned in the heavenly wisdom. We understand the right use of the mind and its thoughts, the heart and its emotions, and the body and its functions. We are truly educated when we appreciate the divine plan and have the courage to serve it. Paths of false values are ways of evil, and from these we ask to be delivered. By restating the desire for inner discernment, we strengthen our own resolutions to grow and unfold. Through prayer we rededicate the life energies within us, by which we exist and are sustained, to the service of the Divine. Our position is negative because we are striving to emerge from limitation into freedom. We petition for the discernment which dissolves limitation and makes possible the appreciation of essential truth.

In its present and accepted form, the Lord's Prayer ends with the paean of praise: "For thine is the kingdom, and the power, and the glory, forever. Amen." This conclusion is not included in some of the older versions, and may be considered as a tribute of adoration. It is the solemn acknowledgement that God is all in all, the eternal ruler, the everlasting strength, and the supernal light. The mystic experiences the kingdom, the power, and the glory as the fullness of God in his own heart. He knows by the faculties of his soul that which is locked within the treasury of light and what flows forth when the doors of the treasure house are open. The Lord's Prayer is one realization expressed by a sevenfold formula. In the heart of the worshiper, the separate sections are mingled into one sublime overtone which envelops the heart and mind in a perfect atmosphere of sanctity.

In prevailing usage, this prayer is a simple act of devotion. The mystical implications are not even known to exist. Even so, the repetition of beautiful words which convey a gentle and loving thought has some effect. The subconscious part of the human nature accepts the ethical values implied by the words. Jesus warned his disciples against idle and indifferent repetitions of words on the assumption that the sounds themselves had magical powers. While some mystics believe in the value of vibration, we must remember that we are no longer speaking the language in which the prayer was given. If it had some remarkable virtue in the Aramaic, we cannot assume that these vibratory tones are preserved in the English translation. It is the better part of wisdom to seek mystical content and become aware of the gifts of the spirit.

All religions have prayers or other meditation formulas for the use of the devout. These simple statements of faith have brought peace and contentment to human hearts everywhere. The kingdom of heaven seems a little nearer in those quiet moments when we seek communion with our heavenly Father.

The mystic discovers that the mood which accompanies prayer lingers after the ritual has been concluded. The consecrated life is itself the perfect tribute to God. As words become deeds and daily living is made serene by the convictions of the soul, the human being is transformed into an embodiment of prayer. Just as religion without the works of faith is only a doctrine, so prayer without deeds is only a fragment of ritualism. The perfect prayer is the perfect life, but this is not yet possible, so we combine the best that we are and the best that we know of consciousness and faith.

The modern world associates prayer with emergency. We become devout only at such times as our own frailties are most evident. Jesus was especially mindful of children because they accept completely what the adult accepts only in part. The child in prayer is able to believe that its words and thoughts are known to a kind and loving parent. Later, a division takes place in the mind. Visible things are grouped together as certainties, and all that lies beyond the sensory perceptions is held to be uncertain. Faith is afflicted with doubts that give rise to questions, which, in turn, lead to further doubts. Even among the devout there is no clear insight into the mysteries of the spirit. Only the experience of personal insufficiency brings the mind back to the acceptance of the divine presence. The intellectual part of man is not actually opposed to the mystical mood. The mind will not deny what the heart commands. The inconsistencies between thought and emotion belong on the level of opinionism. Men and women of brilliant mental attainment have never found it necessary to apologize for their faiths, nor have they regarded prayer as inconsistent with advanced scientific or philosophic attainments.

The ancients believed that at certain seasons of the year, hours of the day, and in parts of the religious rites, the world of gods and men came very near together. They had special rituals and festivals for these occasions and sought through their devotions to know inwardly the exaltation of these blessed moments. The Christian mystic believes that the power of God is peculiarly available during the celebration of the sacraments and during religious reverie. As he opens his heart in prayer, striving with the fullness of his soul to realize the presence of his God, the mystic feels within himself a meeting and mingling of heaven and earth. Some have been privileged to see beyond the veil; others, to hear the music of the spheres. The majority, however, simply know in their hearts by a more subtle faculty. This knowing fills them with a dynamic quality of peace. This is not a quietude which inclines to repose, but a silence full of life. From this peace comes the courage to do and to dare and the wisdom to remain silent. We are spiritually unconquerable because we have overcome fear of that unknown which is our hope and our salvation. As love conquers fear, so life conquers death, and the kingdom of God comes upon the earth.

Chapter Seven

THE BEATITUDES

The Sermon on the Mount is given in St. Matthew, 5-7. The Sermon opens with nine declarations beginning with the words: "Blessed are . . . " These declarations are called the Beatitudes, or blessed statements. Most of the teaching given by Jesus on this occasion is derived from the Old Testament, but cannot be considered as exclusively Jewish in origin. Doctrinal parallels may be found in most of the religions of the East and in the ethical codes of the philosophical systems of the Greeks and Egyptians. The moral instructions of the Master did not conflict with the Jewish law. St. Clement (1st century A.D.) who is said to have been the first of the Apostolic Fathers and a disciple of St. Peter, says in the *Recognitions*: "Between us who believe in Jesus, and the Jews who do not believe on him, there is no difference except as to whether this Jesus is the prophet whom Moses foretold."

The universal distribution of certain basic spiritual convictions justifies the belief that these convictions are sustained by human experience and are not dependent upon the authority of inspired religious leaders. History reveals the effects of conduct and moral codes upon the essential well-being of individuals and groups. The teachings set forth in the Beatitudes constitute an enlightened policy for living. It would be no exaggeration to say that this is the most practical outline of immutable principles yet discovered by mankind. In spite, however, of inspired authority and human experience, these beautiful instructions have never been permitted to dominate or guide the management of mundane affairs. Though honored and respected, they have not been applied in those times or upon those occasions when they would have been most useful.

Strong men are seldom moved by gentle motives, and we have depended upon strength rather than upon integrity for leadership. Opportunism and ambition have formed and reformed nations and have established the precedence which later inspired the multitude. We remain convinced that the way of heaven is apart from the way of earth, and that these extremes cannot meet on common ground. If the human destiny could be completed in the material sphere, we might be justified in our program of so-called realism. But man comes from the unknown, lingers for a time in this vale of uncertainty, and returns to the unknown. He is here for a little while, and elsewhere for an incalculable period of time. No concept of life which does not consider the "elsewhere" condition of human consciousness can be sufficient or satisfactory. Even though we may ultimately integrate the material phase of our living and attain a utopian social system, we have accomplished only in part. The person must achieve a security which cannot be considered by the state of his world. Theoretically at least, man can perfect society because he is the dynamic agent, but society cannot perfect man.

Great legal codes, like those of Hammurabi and Justinian, were devised originally to protect and advance those ethical convictions, the practical value of which was already evident and demonstrable. The overtones of these codes are now known as *laws in equity*, principles of justice which transcend the formal interpretation of statutes and regulations. Law is fulfilled in justice, as learning is fulfilled in understanding. Laws are made by men, but justice is administered by divine agency. Thus justice from the heart tempers with mercy the severities of legal procedure. The spirit conquers the letter to the degree that consciousness ennobles intellect.

The Beatitudes emphasize the very virtues we are least inclined to cultivate. We cannot keep this code and achieve that brittle success which passes as sophistication. As we read these declarations, we may resent the spirit of humility, kindness, and renunciation which pervades the Sermon on the Mount. If we live these teachings of Jesus faithfully and lovingly, we may appear weak and insignificant in the eyes of our contemporaries. When selfishness is fashionable, unselfishness is penalized. A decision must be made. What is the more important to us, that we shall be admired by the foolish, knowing in our own hearts that we are not admirable, or shall we keep faith with ourselves? All honorable religious systems require that the individual make his own choice, weighing all things and clinging to that which is good. It is this honest selection which bestows the courage to keep faith with the divine plan.

When mysteries of the spirit are restricted by words, the words themselves cannot be accepted literally. We must seek those overtones which letters and syllables imprison within their lines and characters. We may read the words with our eyes or hear them with our ears, but we must understand them with our hearts and experience them as mysteries of consciousness with the powers of the soul. Popular usage often obscures the meanings of familar terms impelling us to accept common definitions. In religious practices, we have disfigured nearly all the sayings of the illumined. We have tried to reduce the mystical content of teachings so that they justify prevailing opinions. As a result, we have lost the keys to the Scriptures, and have made other keys which will not fit the lock.

Jesus ascended into a mountain and seated himself. His disciples gathered about him and he taught them, and his words were simple and beautiful with the wisdom of the spirit. And he said: "Blessed are the poor in spirit: for their's is the kingdom of heaven." This has been interpreted to mean that the poor in spirit are the meek, but such a reading is unlikely, as meekness is referred to directly in the third Beatitude. According to the Talmud: "Wherever the greatness of God is mentioned in the Scriptures, the love of God for the humble is spoken of." Humility implies freedom from intellectual pride, and, by extension, the recognition of human dependence upon divine strength. The way of God is from faith in self-knowing to faith in God-knowing.

We all have a sense of self-importance. It is not necessarily egotism, but it is certainly egoism. We believe in the paramount significance of ourselves as persons. Our opinions are important. The attitudes which we have developed through the uncertain processes of trial and error have peculiar merits. We are empowered by our own mind with authority to dominate lives, our own and others. We seldom question or doubt these accumulated prerogatives. We are born to be obeyed and to exert influence. Those who resist or resent stand self-convicted before our mind. By this procedure alone, fallacies are perpetuated and the natural growth of others is impeded.

The mystic, as he approaches the veil of his inner temple, becomes more aware that in the presence of God the wisdom of men appears as foolishness. We can experience much and learn little because we do not accept the honorable testimony of events. In these days we are overly impressed by the pronouncements of human authority. As we are so influenced, we desire to influence others. If our spirits are proud, we wish to be honored and obeyed, but if our spirits are humble, we long to honor and obey the sovereignty of good. It seems to me that the poor in spirit are those who have renounced the driving force of personal determinism and are therefore ready to receive into their souls the kingdom of heaven. The Chinese have a saying that a man moved by his own mind wanders in darkness, but the sage finds the light when he permits himself to be moved by heaven. Thus the rich in opinion are the self-moved, and the poor in spirit are the heaven-moved.

No wealth can be more burdensome than a mass of treasured opinions. By these we create philosophies, fashion theologies, reform institutions, and generously offend each other. In the end we must have more opinions to remedy the disasters of those already enforced.

Convinced that we are strong enough to manage our own affairs, we mismanage them with a good hope and shift the blame for failure to an ungrateful humankind. Fearing that we are misunderstood, we misunderstand the laws by which we live, transforming them into the laws by which we die. There is no place for truth in minds and hearts that are satisfied with their own ignorance. Only when the human way ends in tragedy do we awaken to our own shortcomings. In that moment we are the poor in spirit, for we have accepted and recognized our spiritual poverty. Even the religious-minded must recover from the illusion of theology before they can admit that doctrines can be false riches making the mind to be proud.

The second Beatitude reads: "Blessed are they that mourn, for they shall be comforted." This cannot mean that unhappiness and sorrow are in themselves to be cultivated as spiritual virtues. Psalm 51:17 explains the difficulty: "The sacrifices of God are a broken spirit: a broken and a contrite heart, O God, thou wilt not despise." It is evident to all of us that in our days of success we are not inclined to cultivate the powers of the soul. We turn to religion for help when we are no longer able to sustain ourselves by other means. It seems, therefore, that pain and grief break through the artificial barriers of worldliness and bring us back to eternal verities. Sickness has proven to be an orienting agency in numerous cases. When the body is afflicted with pain, we are no longer concerned with our artificial ambitions. Fearing the worst, we take stock of our own natures and seek inwardly for consolation.

The same holds good in the policies of nations. Powerful and dominant States are not inclined to respect weaker peoples, nor examine the programs by which they seek to advance their spheres of influence. Gradually, power is taken from the oppressor and given to the oppressed. Success is the heaviest responsibility that man must bear. Only the truly great can succeed without arrogance and remain humble in the presence of adulation. We improve only when our present courses are inadequate. If, for a moment, we feel that we are secure, we close our minds to learning and our hearts to charitable deeds. This Beatitude emphasizes the wonderful sense of divine presence that abides with those who seek God in their grief. They are indeed blessed, for they come into the presence of the eternal love. When disaster strikes a community, men forget their private grievances and serve friend and stranger alike. Every door is opened to the needy, and all our resources can be instantly commanded. If we are autocratic in pleasure, we are democratic in pain. After the crisis has passed, we return again to the service of self-interest. We conspire against those we have previously assisted. Fraternity gives way to the old accustomed competitiveness, and the spirit of service departs from the environment.

To mourn is to sorrow over loss of some kind. We grieve when loved ones are taken from us. We are profoundly moved by great calamities that bring misery to others of our kind. In time of war we pray for peace, and we ask that the spirit of understanding shall fill our own heart and bring consolation to all hearts that are afflicted. We seem to know that only the spirit can work the wonder of internal peace. What we cannot give of ourselves, we ask of a power greater than ourselves. When we mourn, the divine presence is intimately known, and its consolation immediately felt. It is not the adversity for which we should be grateful, but the testimony which comes through adversity. Perhaps we are more sensitive to internal guidance when the barriers and obstacles of pride and selfishness are temporarily removed.

Considered psychologically, grief lowers the resistance of the mind, for it is an experience that cannot be rationalized. Even while we mourn, we know that we are in the presence of values which cannot be changed by sorrow. The instinct, however, to express ourselves makes grieving an inner emotion drawn forth as a response to some outer circumstance. The quality of our grieving and the relative importance of the objects of our sorrow tell their story about us. A sincere sadness about some unhappy event may be an honorable statement of our own integrity. We seek not to gain, but to give; not to possess, but to release. If the emotion is sincere, it carries with it subtle statements of conviction. It has been said that tears cleanse the soul, as the waters of baptism purify the body. Sorrow implies a degree of understanding, a reaching out of life to share the experience of life. When grief comes to the spiritually dedicated, there comes with it the Comforter. The pain softens, the heart grows a little weary of its sorrow, and after the emotions have expended themselves there is a strange, deep, quiet silence. It is in this silence that consolation from God is known and accepted. For us, then, living as we do in a world of small and intense personal allegiances, emotional pain brings with it an enlargement of our natures by which we come nearer to the fountain of the soul's strength. This is a blessed mystery even though we must come to it by sadness.

The Beatitudes then continue: "Blessed are the meek, for they shall inherit the earth." This is almost a direct quotation from Psalm 37:11: "But the meek shall inherit the earth; and shall delight themselves in the abundance of peace." God's meek are the lowly, who by their very estates have not known intense pride or ambition. They have found contentment in simple things and are glad for the privileges of labor and rest. We seldom hear of them, for they do not emerge as individuals, but form a deep, broad stratum which sustains upon itself the shifting surfaces of social and political policies. These meek always seem to be the victims of the pressures of the selfish and the wilful. Yet of all parts of our complicated culture, they come the nearest to living the faith of their fathers. They are law-abiding and God-loving. Their visions may be limited, their minds unlearned, and their manners deficient in polish, but they keep the faith, and in moments of emergency they preserve the nation. When the great struggle of strong men is finished and the world is weary of its own vanity, the meek shall remain. They shall inherit the battlefield, and they will plow it and restore it to serve the living. Agitators cannot touch the depths of that great body of human beings which can neither be tempted nor bribed nor threatened.

God's meek also include those who have returned out of the illusion of materiality, like the prodigal son journeying back to his father's house. The truly wise, the surely strong, and the really good are always meek. Only the learned fully realize how little they know. Only those in high positions have experienced the vanity of power. With depth comes gentleness, and when we have found the source of our own security, our pride dissolves in humble gratitude. Those obsessed by the delusion of their own importance finally destroy themselves and others of their kind. As General Wolfe said as he stood below the walls of Quebec: "The path of glory leads but to the grave." There shall be wars and rumors of wars and great changes upon the earth. Civilizations shall lock themslves in desperate struggles over territories and ideologies, but in the end God's meek, victims of countless incivilities, shall inherit the kingdom.

The mystics have always been included among the meek of God. Regardless of their stations or their attainments, they have cultivated quiet and simple ways. They have been content to keep the faith in their hearts and serve their fellow men without hope of recognition or reward. Even helpfulness can be selfish, and there can be a strange quality of arrogance concealed beneath what appears to be humility. Once, however, there has been a complete dedication in the heart to God's will, there can be no hypocrisy in conduct. Those truly humble are honorable and devout persons. They are practicing the fruits of an inner experience. Where there is no ulterior motive, no reservation in the heart or mind, but a complete and selfless devotion to truth, there should be no criticism. Today we expect hypocrisy, for many evil deeds are concealed behind the appearances of kindly gestures. We are suspicious of all, including ourselves. We try to see in mysticism some subtle means of satisfying selfishness or egotism. Believing that men are by nature evil, we demand that this evil expose itself, and we wilfully misinterpret the simple virtues of others. This is unfair to them and even more unfair to our own hearts and minds.

The meek should not be interpreted as representing some downtrodden social class or some underprivileged group in the modern pattern for living. The meek are not those who, having little, desire much, but those in whom there is a contentment of spirit regardless of material estate. There is no virtue in living humbly by necessity, but there is a great virtue in living moderately by choice. The Essenes were such a community of gentle people. They were remembered because the quality of their conduct was wonderfully memorable. We know of nothing which they did that was particularly exceptional, but their entire code was generally exceptional. They sought to restore the dignity of man in Nature by living as human beings should live as comrades, friends, and brethren. By elevating these natural dignities and by cultivating these natural virtues, they fulfilled the obligations of mankind. By freeing themselves from the will to conquer, they relieved the earth of a little of that selfishness with which mortals have chosen to afflict their kind. Those who stand in the presence of the spirit, being neither servile nor arrogant, but deeply humble and eternally grateful, are God's meek.

The Master then declared: "Blessed are they which do hunger and thirst after righteousness, for they shall be filled." Here, again, the thought is derived from the Psalms of David. Psalm 15: 1, 2 reads: "Lord, who shall abide in thy tabernacle? who shall dwell in thy holy hill? He that walketh uprightly, and worketh righteousness, and speaketh the truth in his heart." There are several references in the Old Testament to the gate of the Lord through which only the righteous can enter. The word *righteousness* conveys the meaning of complete integrity. It is a state of godliness free from all guilt or wrong or sin. It carries the further implication of equity and prudence, and, most of all, the performance of action in complete accordance with moral and spiritual wisdom. It is therefore both a state or quality and a kind of conduct or performance consistent with virtue.

To hunger and thirst after righteousness is to consider the moral requirements of consciousness as equal to the physical requirements of the body. Without food and water, we perish physically; and without the quest for righteousness, the soul is without nutrition. When we are in need of food, we are guided in search of nutriment by a pressure within ourselves which we call instinct. The search for truth must be as natural and inevitable as the instinct for survival in the material world. It is not enough that we decide that learning is an ornament of the mind or gentleness an adornment of the heart. The divine source of ourselves is the very substance of existence and growth. Only when we long to return to the conscious at-one-ment with God are we established in righteousness. To do good work, we must know what is good; to be virtuous, we must understand virtue; to be wise, we must apperceive the principle of wisdom, not with the mind alone, but with the instruments of the soul. Until the mystical experience unfolds the divine plan through ourselves, we cannot be wholly righteous. Jesus implied this when he told his disciples that only the Father is good. We increase in goodness as we increase in the presence of God.

The state of righteousness is the condition of harmony, and this in turn bears witness to a perfect adjustment between the divine plan and the human purpose. We are only righteous when conflict between self-will and divine will has been overcome, and we live in a state of conscious obedience. In Isaiah, 33:15, 16, the prophet declares: "He that walketh righteously... shall dwell on high." *To walk* means, in this sense, to proceed through life, to continue day by day to follow in the path that leads to union with the divine nature.

There is the sense of abidance or existence in a quality of inspired labor and dedication to the service of the universal plan. The mystical longing for the intimate realization of truth and love is confirmed by right action.

Jesus then taught: "Blessed are the merciful, for they shall obtain mercy." An old Jewish writing, the Treatise Schabbath, seems to have influenced this Beatitude. The Treatise contains the following lines: "Whosoever hath mercy on men, on him also hath God mercy. But he who showeth no mercy to men, neither to him will God show mercy." The word *mercy* is defined as forbearance under provocation, or the compassionate treatment of an adversary. It is the disposition to forgive and, by extension, the impulse to assist the unfortunate. In mysticism, mercy is a manifestation of compassion and arises from a deep internal experience of human frailty which is accepted without the reaction of offense. Divine mercy is called *grace*, and originates in the divine love. It is natural and proper that love should impel clemency, not because it is required by the moral code, but is an inclination impelled by understanding.

Normal human beings are naturally inclined to be considerate of each other. Superficial policies and artificial inducements may cause the mind and even the heart to nourish resentments. While we are critical and intolerant, we close our inner lives to the blessings of peace and love. The injury that we do to another actually depletes our own moral resources. We are warned by the Scriptures that the cultivation of virtues in order that we may appear to greater personal advantage among our associates is without merit. It is as difficult for the enlightened to hold a grudge as it is for the ignorant to dispose of one. Criticism originates in a nature itself confused and uncertain. Because of the conditioning pressures from our environment, which are stronger than the convictions of conscience, we are prone to criticize and condemn on the slightest provocation. The habit of negative analysis dominates many lives. Once we have permitted suspicions and doubts to grow and flourish in our thinking processes, we find that they cater to our own negative instincts. It is easy to make ourselves miserable by interpreting the moods and actions of our friends and neighbors unkindly. We become censors over private and public morals, and before long we feel impelled to share our conclusions with those of like minds. The result is gossip and slander, which endanger reputations and injure both the guilty and the innocent. We often contact persons who have made careers out of defaming character. They seem to live only to share misery. Nature penalizes such misuse of functions and faculties, and the critic, in the end, suffers more than his victims.

The natural tendency to be merciful is a wonderful cleansing agent. It increases optimism, protects happiness, overcomes doubt, and vanquishes fear. Our abilities, freed from their negative pursuits, are more available for constructive endeavor. Criticism is habit-forming, and if the tendency is tolerated, it increases rapidly until no part of life is safe from its insidious influence. From criticizing a few, we pass rapidly to that state of mind which condemns all. We will be better persons if we seek good with the same enthusiasm with which we are resolved to ferret out evil.

Religion teaches men to love the good and to serve all who are striving after truth. That we shall fall short of perfection is taken for granted. We know how difficult it is to preserve inner integrity when adverse circumstances arise. It is easy to excuse and explain our own faults by the simple statement that the flesh is weak. Common sense should tell us that other human beings are likewise afflicted and are likely to make the same wrong decisions. If we really accept life lovingly and sympathetically, we shall expect no more of our friend or relative than we are able to practice in our own living. We free our temperaments from the habit of criticism by establishing personal consciousness on a higher level of values. We must outgrow immature habits even as we seek maturity of mind and heart. The light of truth illumines dark and confused ways and bestows a larger appreciation for sincere human effort even if this effort is not always obviously sufficient.

The physician comes not to the well, but to the sick. Man's need is man's opportunity. There would be little worth-while to be done if each individual were completely adequate. We are gathered here with the privileges of serving, loving, and understanding each other. This requires some effort and a continued devotion, but we grow most rapidly as we give most abundantly of our own patience and affection. It is better to help than to hurt; it is wiser to accept the injuries than to return them in like measure. When the powers of the soul are strengthened and unfolded, we cannot be moved by the machinations of our enemies. It is our own weakness and not the strength of adversity that is our undoing. It is useless to blame others and criticize their conduct. We are responsible to ourselves *for* ourselves, and no more.

To abide in the grace of God is to dwell in the mercy of the Most High. We consider the act of mercy

as an attribute of the divine nature. We ask to be for-
given for our shortcomings, and fondly expect that our
petition will be acceptable. We approach Divinity by
becoming like in quality with the attributes of Deity.
If, therefore, we abide in the light of God's love, we
manifest this love through our own labors and endeavors. We practice the ways of truth, and by so doing
experience the substance of truth. We can never really
know that which is different from our own natures.
Criticism is different from mercy and is less commendable; therefore, criticism cannot know mercy or justify
it or even desire it. But the human soul, desirous of experiencing the mercy of God, is inspired to transmute
censorship into compassion and in this way becomes
capable of experiencing the divine grace. This grace
is blessedness of the spirit, and they are blessed, indeed,
who bless with their deeds.

The next Beatitude reads: "Blessed are the pure in
heart, for they shall see God." Of all these beautiful
declarations, this is the most completely mystical. It
defines and describes the very substance of that spiritual conviction which has inspired devout men and wom-
en to depart from worldliness and cling to God. Purity
is not only freedom from moral sin, but a state resulting
from the transmutation of all ulterior motives. When
there is no selfishness, no ambition, and no fear in the
human heart, all of the outer works of man will be
good. Sometimes the impurities in our motives are so
subtle and intangible that they pass unrecognized.

It may even happen that we consider certain faults
to be virtues because of wrong ethical instructions. One
of the reasons why so many modern intellectuals are
restless and discontented is that they are afraid to face

internal evaluation of conduct. We all know when our motives are corrupt, but are not always ready to admit the fact even privately. It seems easier to turn our attention to superficial interests and to ignore that which would otherwise plague conscience. In daily experience, hundreds of persons have come to me with their woes. Some have failed in business; others have failed in their homes; still others have failed in health. It is interesting that we should say that a man fails in business rather than that the business has failed him. Even in language there are truths of common usage well worth noting. Almost invariably, those who have been cheated, betrayed, or exploited were the victims of their own ulterior motives.

One victim of himself will say: "I tried to be happy, and I am miserable." Another will explain: "I sacrificed everything for wealth, and now I am poor and sick." So the stories go, and the unfortunates who bring them never recognize that as the motives are bent, so the results are inclined. Resolved to fulfill selfish purposes at all cost, the impure of heart find the cost greater than the reward. Many who believe themselves to be the victims of the dishonesty of their fellow men are really victimized by their own cupidity. In Nature, honest effort is rewarded according to ability. Slight endeavor brings slight gain, but this is not satisfactory to ambitious mortals. Giving as little as they can, they seek to gain all, and finally lose everything.

Purity is required as an experience of consciousness for those dedicated to religious mysticism. In Psalm 24:3, 4, it is written: "Who shall ascend into the hill of the Lord? or who shall stand in his holy place? He that hath clean hands and a pure heart." Here the heart symbolizes the inner life, and the hands, the outer works of man. The instruction given by the Psalmist has only one possible interpretation. Many sects have emphasized different moral codes as being peculiarly acceptable to God. Some have believed that purity could be induced by asceticism, renunciation, and detachment from all worldly instincts and earthly possessions. Others more wisely have realized that virtue is a spiritual strength and must be developed by courageously meeting the difficulties of each passing day. Innocence may be the result of ignorance, but virtue is perfected through wisdom and understanding. We grow, not by avoiding evil, but by rising victoriously over the weaknesses of our flesh.

Good works, even when impelled by conviction or conscience, cannot substitute for delinquencies in other parts of the personality. It is not uncommon to find an individual overworking a single virtue, hoping thereby to compensate for a dozen vices. By this procedure, we are likely to select our pattern of nobility from some department of our living which least interferes with our dominant intemperances. Even our repentances are burdened with schemes, and simple, honorable action unselfishly motivated is comparatively rare. The pure in heart have chosen the path of faith fully realizing the importance of their decision. They are resolved to think straight and to live straight. They know in their hearts that happiness, contentment, and security depend upon inner integrity. As Confucius said: "My doctrine is simple, but its application is not easy." The rules of living are few, and knowledge of them is available to all who seek, but only the one whose strength is great because his heart is pure can keep the law.

The most controversial of the Beatitudes reads: "Blessed are the peacemakers, for they shall see God."

The line "love peace, and seek it at any price" is attributed to the great Rabbinical scholar, Hillel. With conflict the dominant keynote in modern human relationships, the peacemaker is given slight consideration. He may be branded politically as a pacifist or accused of cowardice. We have long held that it is proper to maintain belligerently and aggressively both our principles and our opinions. Failure to do so is diagnosed as deficiency of character. In spite of this, however, the long memory of the world still honors the men of peace and those kindly sages who courageously lived and died in defense of the right to be kind.

The Beatitude tells us that those who make peace shall be given the inner power to know God. Much more seems to be implied. Often those who would bring peace to nations have not found repose within themselves. The strength of those who preach concord comes from the experience of stillness in the heart. Unless the interior faith is established in love, we can speak of peace, but we cannot reveal it or release it through the channels of our natures. It is a well-known fact easily demonstrable that tranquillity of the spirit enriches character and protects the mind in time of trouble. We will be healthier, happier, and more successful in all our undertakings if there is peace in our hearts.

Living as we do in a social system becoming more intense and confused every day, we are constantly tempted to become involved in the conflicts of those around us. We are expected to take sides, to defend and offend, to argue and debate, and most of all to appear appropriately disturbed. It is a social error to be composed when others are exhausting their resources in pointless agitation. To such contestants, the peacemaker is not blessed, for he reveals a measure of self-control, which is itself disquieting to the uncontrolled. Peacemaking is not a profession; it is an instinct, and only succeeds when it is sustained by other gentle and kindly traits of character. When calmness pervades the atmosphere, radiating from a relaxed, well-poised person, it is a force to be reckoned with, but when it is demanded or required by some moralizer who knows not whereof he speaks, it has no calming influence.

We cannot think of peace without reflecting upon the ages. We devoutly desire that the spirit of concord will descend upon the nations and that they will perfect a plan for the arbitration of their differences. This plan also must come from within the leaders of countries. It cannot be bestowed or guaranteed by international law until the humanity in man triumphs over selfishness and ambition and mortal hates are transmuted by the wisdom of experience into immortal love. This process cannot be hastened, but already there is evidence that the human soul, weary of discord, is laying the inner foundation for the outer reformation of mankind.

The dream of peace, the patient dedication to the works of peace, and the devout conviction that peace is attainable and shall be accomplished -- these bear witness to the maturing of mankind. All that has been accomplished in this world has been made possible by dreams and by the patient labor which has built solid foundations under dreams. Each day a few of this earth's vast population feel a growth of peace within themselves. They begin to understand the dimensions of both the disaster and the remedy. Tranquillity, by making possible a better way of life for individuals, reveals its larger purpose and the blessings of universal concord. Those who have found peace have experienced

God in peace, even as the disciples received the gift of peace from Jesus.

The Master then taught: "Blessed are they which are persecuted for righteousness' sake, for their's is the kingdom of heaven." In this declaration, those who have suffered at the hands of the ignorant and the selfish are given consolation. In a materialistic world-pattern, it is the fate of the gentle that they shall suffer from the conspiracies of the cruel. It has been ever thus. We have persecuted the prophets and done evil to those who came to us in love.

Fortunately, it is not necessary for the good man to be understood or appreciated. The mystic knows that the wonderful miracle which takes place within his nature more than compensates for the ingratitude of his fellow men. It is only when we try to live something which we have not actually known or experienced that we are left without the consolation of the spirit. Faith must be complete or it cannot sustain us through years of tribulation, but if it is complete, the tribulation is of appearance rather than of substance. It may appear to others that we are sorely afflicted, because under like conditions they would have no security.

When we live the popular conceits, we are accepted by those around us as like themselves. This acceptance brings with it a measure of sympathy and forbearance, but to enjoy this kind of security we must sacrifice the larger and more permanent values. If we choose to follow the way of the spirit, we depart from the approval of the majority of our contemporaries. We are no longer understood, but walk as strangers. Even our own families and the friends of a lifetime cannot bridge the interval which separates purposed living from a purposeless existence. We all misunderstand that which we do not understand. We are unwilling to accept a mystery, but must solve it according to the knowledge available to us.

We see a friend departing from ways of easy living into what appears, by our estimation, to be a fruitless striving after unattainables. He seems to be more and more alone, and we give thanks that we are still part of the herd and can share both its fortunes and misfortunes. If we observe that the truth seeker is sacrificing his economic security or is contenting himself with few possessions, we feel that he is foolishly depriving his nature of such luxuries as most of us accept as necessities. Ultimately, it seems to us that the devout mystic brings down upon himself the antagonism of public opinion. He is ostracized, publicly censured, and privately ridiculed, and as a proof that he is wasting his life, we point to his diminishing goods and growing indifference to the psychosis of success. If such a one had lived in earlier times, he might have been a martyr to the whims of some despotic prince or the irritated clergy, but now he is exposed only in the arena of public opinion, where his devotion to principles amuses the thoughtless.

Seen from the outside, the mystic is an unfortunate enthusiast, more to be pitied than to be blamed. The worldly-wise give thanks that they have escaped a similar destiny, and continue in such complacency as they are able to maintain. As the mystic advances on his own course, however, he passes from the small reactionary sphere into an ever-larger universe. Light increases within him, and it would not be proper to say that he suffers a sense of loss or deprivation. He experiences rather a constant realization of gain; he becomes more, even as he seems to possess less. He is exchanging an

old way of life walked in darkness for a new way of
life walked in light. The presence of God, the increasing
awareness of the wonders of the divine nature, and the
blessed consolation of the spirit reward him for renounc-
ing conflict and death.

The one sorrow of those who are great of vision is
that they cannot share what they have experienced with
those they love. Each must grow for himself and we
cannot bestow maturity of soul any more than we can
force the maturity of body. The mystic is always a
teacher by both word and example, but he learns what
Jesus knew: that the world still rejects the man of soul,
and glorifies the man of body. But there are always a
few in whose hearts the seeds fall upon good ground.
Mystics have exercised a greater influence than they
knew. Soul-hunger seeks its own nutrition and finds as
much as it can take in the lives and words of the world
teachers and prophets.

The last of the Beatitudes extends this concept and
explains the inner mystery: "Blessed are ye when men
shall revile you and persecute you, and say all manner
of evil against you falsely, for my sake. Rejoice, and be
exceeding glad: for great is your reward in heaven: for
so persecuted they the prophets that came before you."
We must understand heaven not as a future state, but
as used in this text it signifies the inner life in God.
Heaven is the quietude of the spirit, the abode of internal peace, the rest that comes to the soul after it has
accepted the way of righteousness.

The man of soul, who is the personification of the
enlightened conviction of consciousness, comforts the
mind and the heart and prepares them to receive the
disdain of mortals. If we are to be true to the divine
power within us, we must endure all things for its sake.

We must also, however, accept persecution with love, false witness with humility, and all indignities with gentleness of heart. We receive these revilings without complaint because we are in the service of that which is older than the world and which will endure when time is no more. We have chosen, and there is no regret. We have found a work worthy of our talent and a dream that consoles the spirit. It is enough that we are good and faithful servants of that eternal plan that must ultimately succeed when the works of selfishness and ambition have failed.

The internal mystery of the Christian faith is the presence of the Master as the real, though invisible, power. We accept his authority and become citizens of his kingdom. We live according to his laws and keep his commandments, and we are not afraid. The best part of ourselves has found its destiny, and has returned home from exile in a world of form. There is nothing that the dedicated heart is not ever ready to accomplish in the name of the keeper of the light. The labarum shines in the sky above the mortal battlefield. By this sign the aspiring soul conquers the ages and becomes one with truth.

THE IMMACULATE CONCEPTION IN THE HUMAN SOUL

Chapter Eight

THE DIVINE TRAGEDY

The events in the life of the Master from Friday, the
15th of Nisan (April 7th) to Sunday, the 17th of Nisan
(April 9th) consummated his ministry. The drama unfolded with the fatality of happenings predestined and
foreordained. Even the words attributed to Jesus were
carefully selected from older sources, thus giving them
peculiar weight and authority. In St. Matthew, 26:30,
it says that after the Last Supper Jesus and the disciples
sang a hymn. Most Bible commentators have assumed
that this was part of the Hallel, or song of praise, con-
sisting of sections taken from the Psalms. It seems more
probable that the fragments of a religious song preserved in the two hundred thirty-seventh letter of St.
Augustine to the Priscillian bishop, Ceretius, are from

181

the actual hymn which Jesus and his disciples sang
together. The words are as follows:

I wish to unbind, and I wish to be unbound.
I wish to save, and I wish to be saved.
I wish to beget, and I wish to be begotten.
I wish to sing; dance ye all with joy.
I wish to weep; be ye all struck with grief.
I wish to adorn, and I wish to be adorned.
I am the lamp for you who see me.
I am the gate for you who knock.
Ye who see what I do, do not tell what I am doing.
I have enacted all in this discourse,
And I have not been in any way deceived.

One of the apocryphal gospels includes the statement that Jesus and his disciples performed a sacred
dance after the Last Supper. The ritual of breaking
bread and sharing a cup existed among the ancient Jews
and is mentioned in connection with the Mithraic cult
of Persia and the ceremonies performed by Pythagoras
at Delphi. After the Paschal supper, the master of a
Jewish family shared bread and wine with the members
of his household, including the servants, as a token of
brotherly love and esteem. This would agree with the
beautiful words spoken by Jesus on the occasion. He
signified that his disciples were not his servants but his
brothers, and the sermon enlarges the concept of the
sacrament.

It was held by the early mystical theologians of the
Christian faith that the cup of Gethsemane, to which
Jesus resigned himself, contained not the bitter potion
of death, but the poison of the mortal sins of mankind
committed against the will of God. Here the mystery
of the Christos, the sinless son of the eternal Father, is

strongly intimated. After the agony in the garden, Jesus said: "The hour is at hand, and the Son of Man is betrayed into the hands of sinners." The acceptance of the chalice of sorrow was the acknowledgment by the Master of the destiny required by the world drama. After this final pledge of obedience, Jesus patiently bore the indignites and injustices that were heaped upon him.

The curious episode of the release of Barabbas is an integral part of the sacred symbolism. Pilate was apparently convinced that Jesus was innocent of any serious offense. He did not expect to influence the group which was resolved upon the death of the religious teacher. The Roman statesman, however, hoped to appeal to the people of Jerusalem who so recently had regarded Jesus as their hero. Pilate, seeking to placate all parties, proposed to release the great prisoner because it was usual to perform such an action on the day of feasting. Pilate was further induced to make this move by a warning which had been sent to him by his wife, who had been troubled by a dream. The Roman procurator offered to release either Jesus or Barabbas, and the multitude cried out in favor of Barabbas.

It appears, by a strange coincidence, that this criminal, who for sedition and murder had been cast into prison, was also named Jesus and surnamed Barabbas, meaning *son of the father*. The first name of this man has been removed from most of the older manuscripts. One Biblical commentator thus examines the decision of the people: "The choice was offered them between one who had broken the laws of God and man, and One who had given his whole life up to the doing good and speaking truth amongst them. They condemned the latter to death, and were eager for the deliverance of the former." By rejecting the son of heaven and

choosing as their hero a robber, murderer, and insur-
rectionist, they proclaimed their allegiance to darkness.
The world tragedy bears witness to that part of human
nature which has always chosen the lesser in the presence of the greater. The man of soul was sacrificed to the worldly
ambitions of the unregenerate man of flesh. Nor did
this persecution expend its fury outside the walls of
Jerusalem. The sacrifice is perpetual. It recurs in the
daily decisions of countless persons who regard themselves as honorable. They betray principles in order
to advance their policies and ambitions. The light in
the heart, which is to become the light of the world, is
denied, and, with only passing reservations, we accept
Barabbas and confer upon him privileges and high
estate. We are appropriately rewarded by war, crime,
and death. The human code of ethics, typified by Pilate,
is powerless to resist the will of the majority. When it
advises moderation, the body politic cries out: "If thou
let this man go, thou art not Caesar's friend."

The indefinite references in the Gospels indicate
that Golgotha was a place of execution outside the city
of Jerusalem. The word literally means *a skull*, but
three of the Evangelists described it as the "place
of a skull." In St. Luke, the name *Calvary* is introduced
by the translators, who use *calvaria*, i.e. *a bare skull*.
The use of the word *mount* in connection with Calvary
has no support from the older texts. The best available
explanation is that Golgotha was a slight elevation, so-
named because it was skull-shaped. It was not a place
of bones, because Jewish law forbade that these be
left unburied. There is a legend that the skull of Adam
was buried at Golgotha, and that the cross on which
the Master was crucified was raised over this relic of

the first man. This may explain the presence of the skull at the base of many old crucifixes.

We can disregard the uncertainties of the Biblical narratives, and pass to the study of the religious symbolism. The unfoldment of the mystery drama causes Jesus to die upon the cross at the place called Golgotha. It was here that the soldiers divided his garments and cast lots for them. This fact fulfilled Psalm 22: 18: "They part my garments among them, and cast lots upon my vesture." At the ninth hour (3:00 P.M.) Jesus spoke with a loud voice the opening words of the 22nd Psalm: "My God, my God, why hast thou forsaken me?" After he had received the sponge of sour wine, he spoke again: "It is finished." St. Luke gives as the last words of Jesus: "Father, into thy hands I commend my spirit." This is the first part of the fifth verse of the 31st Psalm. It is evident that these exact quotations were more than the natural utterances of a dying man. They bind together a vast concept which is the key to the mystery.

Secret sects of the Lebanon taught quite openly a doctrine of internal salvation founded upon the eternal sacrifice. It was their interpretation which later deeply influenced St. Paul. These mystics knew from within themselves that the doctrine of the Christos was the vestment which should be parted and the seamless robe for which the soldiers should cast their lots. Divided by interpretation, the secret teaching was lost to the world and could be restored only in the hearts of the devout. It is not without reason and just cause that all the great religions of the world have announced the coming of the Messiah. Each has expected him to appear from within its own communion, and all have identified the event with the appearance of their own prophet or inspired leader. In this way, a mystery, though divided doctrinally, is undivided substantially.

The spiritual quickening of the human race by divine power is apperceptively known and expected. The conviction arises from the spiritual need of man, who can see no solution to his own insufficiency except divine intercession. As he aspires within himself to a better life and to the practice of those beliefs which are nearest and dearest to him, he experiences a descent of power through himself. It is this conferred resource which is his hope and his salvation. Nor does it appear that this bestowal of grace from the source of life is essentially miraculous. Though wonderful, it is natural, and though the process surpasses understanding, the fact of it is understood. An occurrence which has been known and recorded and about which there are ample records cannot be denied or regarded as incredible. The mystical experience has happened not once, but many times, and the very happening is a promise of other things to come. Doctrinally the advent of the Messiah has been given historical and literal shape and dimension, but mystically it remains an eternal coming of the spirit.

The ancient Egyptians personified universal wisdom as Thoth, or Hermes, and said that he was the author of thirty thousand books. They meant, obviously, that the universal principle of reason was responsible for all illumined writings. One truth is revealed through all the nobler works of men even though this unity is not obvious on the material plane of living. The founders of religion, to the degree that they were sincere and dedicated, were inspired by the same spirit of truth and brought the same message. In each case, the prophet claimed divine inspiration and acknowledged himself to be the servant of an ageless cause. Mohammed in prayer in the cavern on Mt. Hira, Buddha in meditation under the bo tree near Madras, and Zoroaster in his hermitage surrounded by a ring of flames were convinced that they were the instruments of the true God. These noble men had first sought truth with a complete dedication of their lives and their worldly goods. As they advanced along the difficult road, they beheld the radiant appearance coming forth out of the unknown to meet them. They were assured that as devoutly as men long for that which is divine so the heavenly Father longs to be known and found by his creatures.

Some of the Church Fathers believed that God incarnated in his own son, but those of more skeptical minds have rejected the literal implications of such an occurrence. The mystic understands what is meant and knows full well that the sovereignty which maintains the universe could not be locked within the proportions of a man. But God is a spirit with power to be everywhere and in everything, and that which bears witness to the divine life becomes substantially the incarnation or embodiment of that life. The presence of God in some place does not imply the absence of God in other places. The heavenly power meets and embraces all who seek it and bestows itself upon them, entering into them as they enter into it. This mingling is a baptism of the spirit and by the spirit. Let us assume, for a moment, that the unfoldment of life is in the keeping of a wisdom and a love greater than our own. We can examine the evidence which testifies to the growth of man through the ages. Human evolution has been orderly and within a broad, sufficient pattern of natural laws. As his environments changed, the human being developed faculties and functions suitable to his requirements. There was nothing necessary which was not available. Mankind met the challenge of need by releasing from within itself that which was needful. Progress is a magnificent testimony to the internal resources of growing creatures. Each step was slow and difficult, but it was accomplished.

Is man to assume, then, that his future needs, more subtle but no less real, will not be met from within his own potentials? What are these potentials except the availability of all that is good? Is not mysticism the normal extension of growth pressing on toward the production of superior types of beings? Primitive man was satisfied to survive the hazards of his environment. Medieval man aspired to the conquest of the world about him for the glorification of his own sense of power. Modern man would go further. Disillusioned by the disastrous consequences of his own ingenuity, he knows within himself that he can never be secure until he conquers his own internal darkness. Must we consider such a conviction as merely an escape mechanism? If so, why does this urge increase and distribute itself throughout the world, calling devout persons from every walk of life and binding them to a larger concept of destiny?

Mystics have always been persecuted or ridiculed or ignored, but they do not disappear from human society. They are strengthened by the very adversities to which they are subjected. Others follow their examples, sacrificing worldly comforts and security in the search for the overself. Already, advanced scientists are accepting not only the possibility but also the probability that man possesses faculties of knowing and organs of sensory extension superior to those which he

6

now uses. Extrasensory perception has become a respectable subject for investigation. We can no longer reject empirically the mass of evidence that cannot be explained by traditional methods of knowledge. The most certain and rapid method by which the human being can be rescued from his present limited concept will be the growth of means of cognition by which he can reorient himself in the universal pattern.

Most of us have at least one mystical experience during our lifetime. It may not be a wonderful illumination, but it does testify to the existence and availability of resources not generally recognized. Because such occurrences are exceptional and contrary to our normal expectancies, we ignore them or explain them away to our own satisfaction. Extrasensory faculties are nearer to the surface than we are inclined to think. The interventions of these higher instruments of cognition are becoming increasingly frequent, especially among those dedicated to high principles. Washington's vision at Valley Forge, Lincoln's mystical experiences, and Gandhi's emphasis upon the contemplative life have transcended private concern and have contributed to the history of modern times. Identify the man who is dedicated to the improvement of human society and you will find one whose strength of purpose comes from deep and hidden places within himself. This so-called phenomenon is the long shadow of events to come.

If the power to know by internal experience is possible to some, it is potentially possible to all. It is the mystic, and not the hero of science-fiction, who will be the superman of tomorrow. The world is not drifting toward a mechanistic paradise. The motion forward is two motions and not one. The most evident is advancement on the present level, by which man hopes to organize the resources of his planet. The least evident, but the most important, is the enlargement of human consciousness from within itself, by which all external objectives will finally be censored. Our dreams of the future are the extensions of our present hopes. As we change, these dreams will be altered, and the ultimates we now regard or fear are not the final shapes of things to come. They can only happen if we remain as we are, but we are not destined to so remain.

Growth is strange and difficult to estimate because its processes are slow and gradual. Change that is imposed upon us is resented and opposed, but change that comes from within us through gentle promptings is accepted without question. Modern standards of living do not appear unreasonable because a few centuries ago they would have been considered impossible. Materialism cannot be defeated by the mind or disproved by oratory. It is overcome by the gradual opening of internal eyes which understand better as they see more, and vice versa. When faculties of internal knowing are commonly possessed, our way of life will adapt to their implications. We will have new hopes and purposes, new aspirations, and probably new ambitions. These will become the normal expectancies until they, too, are left behind by the ceaseless motion of growth.

The present crisis in human evolution is especially important because it is the first time that we have faced transition from one dimension of the universe to another. Until now we have extended along familiar lines, building visibly upon visible foundations. The time has come to contemplate a difficult and, for most, an incredible change. We must build invisibly upon the old footing, extending from works objective to works subjective. We cannot advance further without the personal and collective experience of universal causes. In some way and by some means, we must cross the line which divides the material and spiritual parts of Nature. We have approached this line gradually, but in the instant of crossing we face a critical adjustment within ourselves. Once we have passed the line, growth can continue in its slow and orderly way as we adjust to the implications of a new kind of existence.

The ancients symbolized that which divides the worlds as a veil, and this is the veil of the temple of Jerusalem that was rent at the moment of the death of Jesus. This line, according to Omar Khayyam, is also the hair which divides the false and the true. *False* does not mean here something wrong or evil, but an appearance which is misunderstood because the cause of it is unknown. It would be most helpful if at this time psychologists and other specialists in the field of man's internal phenomena would consider the possibility that the mystic is the prototype of future humanity and not a forlorn visionary destined to wander his years in an unsympathetic sphere.

The Utopians, from Plato to Defoe, have described new kinds of creatures growing up among men, resembling outwardly their companions and associates, but inwardly set apart for a high destiny. These are the Philosophic Elect, the men of the sunrise, the citizens of an empire of poets and dreamers. They dream true because they are using available extrasensory resources and not their own imaginations. They have always spoken with a strange note of authority because, of all men, they alone know whereof they speak. These heroes, as the Greeks called them, have always crossed the line and are citizens of two states of consciousness. Inwardly they dwell in cause even as outwardly they live in a world of effects.

Rufus M. Jones, Professor of Philosophy, Haverford College, in his article on mysticism in the *Encyclopaedia of Religion and Ethics*, writes: "The mystical experience, especially in the loftiest spiritual geniuses of the race, may very well be the emergence of a new type-level of life, a higher manner of correspondence with ultimate sources of reality, an *elan vital* of the soul, a surge of the entire self towards ineffable fullness of life." Farther in the same article, Dr. Jones adds: "The mystical experience itself, as an inner life-event, is unmistakably one of the great tap-roots of personal religion, bringing, as it does, to the recipient undemonstrable, but at the same time irrefragable, certainty of higher personal life in contact with the personal self, and revealing a superaddition of life-functions and new depth-levels of truth."

The operations of Nature nearly always manifest first by producing isolated examples of processes later to become general. These apparent anomalies gradually increase in number until they establish the new norm. In this way the exceptional is slowly transformed into the usual and acceptable. Mysticism as a teaching affirms the existence and availability of an intuitive power which can be released by contemplation and directed by intensity of moral purpose. The use of this faculty increases its acuteness or power of spiritual penetration. Although comparatively latent in the majority of mankind, vestiges of intuitive power may be noted and observed among the survivors of ancient peoples, and indications of its gradual reactivation may be seen in the more advanced types of contemporary humanity. Nearly always, the soul powers respond to a genuine aspiration toward a superior concept for living. Such aspiration, in turn, is stimulated by the uncertainties of mortal life. There is a forceful restatement of mystical tradition in all periods of emergency.

The present century has been so ridden with pressures and tensions that it can best be described as a continuous emergency. For this distressful state, there is no expectation of immediate relief. The future promises only further misfortune resulting from causes already in motion. Popular interest in the mystical part of religion has increased steadily since the years of World War I. Human consciounesss is resolved to survive the ordeal of environment by expanding its intuitive faculties. Only certainty can overcome uncertainty and release man from the tensions generated by fear and doubt. We know this in our hearts, and when directly challenged we are inspired to act in accordance with our knowledge.

The mystical philosophers of the past not only realized that some day humanity would shift its ethical structure from a physical to a spiritual footing, but also that each individual living in the collective plan would be required to adjust his code and his character to the new culture-level. As this critical hour approaches, it is important that man be supported by a measure of understanding. When we desire to visit a far country, we prepare ourselves for the adventure. We discuss the trip with other travelers, and read accounts of the regions through which we shall pass. If we intend to remain long in another land, we may even study the language and familiarize ourselves with the manners and customs. Never for a moment, however, do we regard this knowledge accumulated from the words and experiences of others as a substitute for our proposed journey. No amount of study can equal the direct impact of personal experience. The same is true in religion. Tradition lowers our resistance to larger concepts, and study makes possible a fuller appreciation for facts later to be known. When new concepts have become acceptable through familiarity, transition from one level of consciousness to another is easier and less violent. We are preserved from the distress which change brings to those of inflexible temperament.

For more than two thousand years we have been taught to expect a wonderful occurrence by which our lives and institutions would be transformed. We dimly perceive the direction of this transformation which is to be revealed as growth in righteousness. Recognized evils will be corrected, and respected virtues will be strengthened. Although we accept the desirability of spiritual progress and rejoice at the benefits which will ultimately accumulate, we are still profoundly disturbed at the prospect of individual or collective reformation. Whatever happens which disturbs the tranquillity or intranquillity of the status quo is regarded with the gravest apprehension. We do not recognize the fact of general progress in any particular event. The moment any policy seems to restrain our selfish and ambitious instincts, we are resentful in our minds and hearts, even though at the same moment our faculties are seemingly united in a prayer for peace and enlightenment.

Education by theoretical means, sustained by the examples of great leaders and demonstrated through the interpretation of natural phenomena, can bring the aspiring soul to the line where opinion ceases and knowledge begins. Instruction is necessary, but can never be complete, nor can it influence those who resist or resent that which is taught. All who teach are attempting to convert by persuasion. They point out the reasonableness of the doctrine they advocate and indicate the benefits which may be expected as the result of allegiance to the new concept. These spiritual opportunities are meaningful only if we stand in need of such opportunities and admit this need to ourselves.

Christian mystics have taught that at the time of the crucifixion a divine power flowed into the material universe. This was symbolized by the blood which dropped from the wounds of Christ into the earth at the foot of the cross. A dimension of consciousness, previously part of the divine nature, entered into the material state so that it could operate from within living creatures as an element in the compound of consciousness. By this intensification of spiritual resources, humanity will be able to take the next great step in its journey toward the Infinite. Because the step is exceptional, the help is likewise extraordinary.

In old symbolism, the cross represented a point of junction of a vertical and horizontal line. It therefore signified the passing over or the crossing from a condition of materiality to a state of spirituality. The ancients said that form was a compound composed of the union of spirit and matter. All forms partake of both energy and substance, for they are matter held in patterns by life, and they are vehicles for the manifestations of living beings. In the philosophic aspects of mysticism, the cross was therefore form, the lines which composed it being the two irreconcilable qualities which are temporarily united. It is on the cross of form that consciousness is crucified. Form may be either the corporeal structure of an atom or the vast physical expanse of the universe. It is a condition rather than an object. Wherever there are forms, there

are limitations upon life, and wherever there is limitation, there is growth manifesting as a motion toward
freedom.

The Greeks believed that the Supreme Being entered
into the processes of creation, voluntarily assuming the
substance of the world even as he generated this substance out of his own nature. The spiritual resource
that was everywhere generally, was at the core of each
living thing particularly. By this circumstance, the
innermost and the furthermost were identical, but were
available only by opening the channels provided by
the evolving powers and faculties of the human soul.
The human being is conscious of himself and he is also
aware of his own body, and can, upon occasion, direct
his attention toward bodily function, often as the result
of physical discomfort. Although man's consciousness
is thus held, it would be incorrect to affirm that he is
unaware beyond the circumference of his physical
form. By faculties within himself, he has attempted
to conquer the material universe, and his ambitions
have been restricted only because he could not escape
from a quality of form even though he ingeniously supplemented his own limitations by mechanical devices.

Mystics have taught that, although the divine power
had entered into its own works to vitalize them and give
them the power to grow and to reproduce their kind,
Deity was not without the full consciousness of its own
works and purposes. The life-principle carried man to
the fulfillment of its own requirements. The vitality of
Deity accomplished the fruitfulness of the earth. It
made forms that were suitable habitations for rational
and enlightened creatures. After these were prepared,
like vessels to receive a greater content, a new part of

the universal entity descended into these bodies repeating the original creation, but this time on the plane of soul power.

In I. Corinthians, 15: 36-50, St. Paul explains the mystery of the incarnation by comparing the death and resurrection of Christ with the mystery of the germination of a seed: "... that which thou sowest is not quickened except it die ... so also is the resurrection of the dead. It is sown in corruption; it is raised in incorruption. ... It is sown a natural body; it is raised a spiritual body. There is a natural body, and there is a spiritual body. And so it is written, the first man Adam was made a living soul; the last Adam was made a quickening spirit. ... The first man is of the earth earthy: the second man is the Lord from heaven."

These statements refer to the ascent of the human consciousness from the state of ignorance to the condition of enlightenment. In the spiritual experience of the mystic, Golgotha is the summit of the mortal state. It is the line which separates the objective condition of man from his subjective life in spirit. The gentle, unselfish, patient search for inner light leads the truth seeker along the Stations of the Cross—the Via Dolorosa. The journey toward becoming is accompanied by a series of releases from the activities of the physical sensory perceptions and faculties. The man who is of the earth earthy is among those who have fallen asleep in Christ. Oriental mystics have the same doctrine, for they seek a state of samadhi, or the extinction of self in a condition of complete selflessness. But those who sleep in Christ have not perished. "But now," writes St. Paul, "is Christ risen from the dead, and become the first fruits of them that slept."

The understanding of these words depends upon the mystical definition of sleep. St. Paul likened sleep to a kind of death which we die daily. At the end of the day we repose ourselves with the fond expectation of rest and refreshment. With a perfect faith which is instinctive, we release ourselves from conscious activity, trusting our lives, with the faith of a little child, to the oblivion which gradually envelops us. After this comes a state of unknowing, a timeless suspension, from which we emerge again in due course and resume the concerns of physical living. As the mind resigns itself physically to sleep, so the human consciousness in its quest for reality enters in perfect faith into the quietude of God. As sleep temporarily terminates all the confusion and conflict of the mind and emotions, it appropriately conveys the meaning of faith.

In order for faith to be real, there must be a complete and unquestioning acceptance of universal integrity. Faith is, therefore, doubt going to sleep in the security of a strong and beautiful conviction. Most human reactions are negative, fearful, and uncertain. As these are transformed and redeemed by the powers of the soul, the old and familiar man, who knew himself only by his uncertainties, fades away, and a new person takes his place.

As we approach the line between the lower and higher states of consciousness, we experience a new definition of faith. The old life groping upward from below finds faith and then experiences the mystical death. This is the corruptible man who is destroyed, not by his sin, but by his virtue. Faith ends the little despotism of self-purpose and all the activities that are powered by the pressures of vanity. The corruptible man has his own philosophy of life, his own convictions, policies, plots, and counterplots. For most of us, he is the real self, for we have known no other nature in the experience of ourselves. He belongs to the kingdom of this world, and if he departs from it he dies, like a fish that has been taken out of water. The institutions which have been built by this corruptible man are themselves likewise corruptible. They are houses standing upon shifting sands, and the days of this man are few and full of troubles.

Within the complex structure of the corruptible man there is an incorruptible seed or, as some have said, a seed sown in corruption. This is the second man of St. Paul who is from heaven and is himself the Lord. Slowly and wonderfully the man from heaven increases and is experienced, not as a source of knowledge or of wisdom or of satisfaction, but as an enlarging benevolent silence forever absorbing into itself the sound and the fury. The irresistible power of the man of heaven strengthens the resolutions of the soul and makes possible the human dedication to the divine plan. As the mystic comes closer and closer to the mystical experience, he knows himself to be sinking, with full and complete confidence, into the repose of God. His humanity goes to sleep in the divine purpose, and by this very action becomes the "first born" of those who slept.

If faith brings the mystical death to those who live in fear, so it makes possible the second birth. The peace of God is both the tomb and the womb, for those who die in the flesh are reborn in the spirit. As mortal ambitions are renounced, immortal aspirations take their places, and as we give up the lesser we receive the greater. Ignorance dies in faith, and wisdom is born of faith. That which is the last part of uncertainty is the first part of certitude. Before we can pass on to that new orientation of faculties which is at hand, we must outgrow certain illusions, and experience previously unrecognized realities. The resurrection occurs through the focusing of consciousness in the universe of causes. Before we can be born in this better quality, we must vigorously detach ourselves from a fixation which will not permit us to escape from the tyranny of the sensory faculties. Those perceptive functions which are useful and necessary in the world of form are unable to convey or even to accept impulses which are beyond the sensory areas of receptivity. If these senses are unable to function on a higher level, then the world to which they bear witness ceases to exist as a reality. It vanishes away as in sleep, and leaves not a wrack behind.

Death is a departure from this world when the body is no longer able to maintain its functions. Faith is a departure from this world when the heart and mind are no longer able to accept the tyranny of matter as part of the divine will. In both cases, the submergence of conscious action is followed, after a time, by a re-emergence. Those who die in the flesh are reborn in the flesh, for, although they have left the world, worldliness has not departed from them. The few who have gone to sleep in faith are reborn from the womb of faith into the world of light. They have experienced the resurrection in the love of the Father and they abide in the grace of the spirit. By material evolution, the first born of earth have evolved painfully from ignorance to faith. By spiritual evolution, the first born in Christ begin a process of unfoldment or qualitative evolution, by which they proceed from faith to truth. Thus faith itself in its two aspects is meat for the men of earth and milk for the babes of heaven.

In the final act of the mystery upon Golgotha, Jesus returned his spirit to the keeping of his heavenly Father and found peace in death. It was then that Joseph of Arimathea asked permission to take the body of the Master and place it in a new tomb. In this loving and charitable deed, Joseph was assisted by Nicodemus. Soldiers were placed to guard the tomb, as there was a fear that the followers of Jesus might attempt to remove his body and then claim that he had risen from the dead. It was on the morning following Sunday, the 17th of Nisan, that the resurrection is reported to have taken place. None of the Evangelists mentioned the exact hour, and there was not anyone present except the soldiers. There was a great agitation and shaking of the earth, and the angel of the Lord descended, and rolled back the stone from the door of the tomb and sat upon the stone. The four Gospels differ considerably at this point of their narratives. The women who had knelt at the foot of the cross had departed to prepare spices for the embalming of the sacred remains. They came early on the first day of the week, but the stone had already been removed and the tomb was empty. Mary Magdalene seems to have assumed that the body had been removed, for she told Peter that the Lord had been taken away.

The original teaching concerning the resurrection of the Master is recorded in I. Corinthians, 15: 3-8: "For I delivered unto you first of all that which I also received, how that Christ died for our sins according to the scriptures; And that he was buried, and that he rose again the third day according to the scriptures: And that he was seen of Cephas, then of the twelve: After that, he was seen of above five hundred brethren at once; of whom the greater part remain unto this present, but some are fallen asleep. After that, he was seen of James; then of all the apostles. And last of all he was seen of me also, as of one born out of due time."

The earliest available reports indicate that the crucified Jesus returned from the kingdom of the dead, not in his former body of flesh and blood, but invested with a new and heavenly body. This explains why St. Paul, on the occasion of his conversion, beheld only a light and yet could say that he had seen Christ. In mysticism, sight is not with the eye of the brain, but with the eye of the heart. The teachings found in the Epistles emphasize that for those who believe in the spirit there is a new body which is prepared in heaven. This point explains the theological difference between the Church militant and the Church triumphant. The radiant vestment of the faithful is the wedding garment mentioned by St. Paul, which is to be worn on the occasion when the ecclesia adorned as a bride is united with the Lamb.

There is an important parallel between the account of the death of Jesus and the last days of Moses. The Promised Land, which Moses was permitted to behold but not to enter, signifies the complete experience of truth. Canaan is the symbol of fulfillment, the reward, the ultimate goal, the end which justifies the long and difficult disciplines of self-unfoldment. The Lord of all things, when he fashioned the world, created fifty gates of wisdom. Moses, the servant of the Lord, passed through forty-nine of these gates, but through the fiftieth gate he could not pass. Greatness of learning makes it possible for man to stand upon a mountain and look across toward the substance of eternity, but final union with the Supreme Mystery is beyond even wisdom.

According to the mystical tradition, mortal mind goes to sleep in the divine mind, passing in this way from an earthly to a heavenly state. Through the cultivation of knowledge and the practice of good works, we enlarge in understanding. Upon the crest of the world, whether it be Moab, Golgotha, or Himavat, there is that supreme moment when the wisdom of man surrenders to the grace of God. This is the instant that changes the world. Time returns to eternity; the part is united with the whole; the spark is one again with the flame. The resurrection which follows immediately witnesses the triumph of the man of soul. The Holy Sepulcher so long in the hands of the infidel is the human personality, bound for ages by the tyrannies of ignorance and fear.

As the man of earth in the earth suspires, so the man of heaven to the sphere of grace aspires. In the Ascension, the son of heaven returns to his Father to reign in glory over the quick and the dead—the enlightened and the unenlightened. The mystic understands the Ascension not as a historical event only, but as the unfolding of evolutionary processes on the plane of consciousness. As man ascends physically through the levels of growth and culture recognized by anthropologists, so he rises spiritually through the mysteries of the hierarchy as described in the writings of seers and saints. Materially he grows in darkness toward the light; spiritually he grows in light toward the source of universal light.

Intuitively known by consciousness itself, the crucifixion of Jesus is the travail which precedes the mystical birth. It was written that Melchizedek, King of Salem, was his own father and his own mother. This explains the symbolism of the phoenix reborn from its own body. Love of God and unselfish service in the spirit of truth strengthen our determination to make the final and complete renunciation of ourselves to the eternal will. In that moment, we give the last full measure of devotion. We give not only of ourselves, but all that we are, reserving nothing, not even an existence apart from truth. In this way, we go to sleep in the bosom of Abraham and rest with our fathers.

When we awaken, we have crossed the line that divides the outer and inner worlds. We then understand why we gain all by giving all. We have passed not to some airy paradise, but into conscious knowledge of the universal wonder. As we learn to see with the eyes of the soul, we awaken from the mystery of death. We are born again, but we are not the same. In us, all things have changed, and we abide in hope, faith, and love, and the greatest of these is love.

EARLY PORTRAIT OF ST. PAUL

Chapter Nine

CHRIST, THE SON OF GOD

Such biographical facts as are available about St. Paul were gleaned from The Acts of the Apostles and the Pauline Epistles. If we are prepared to assume that The Acts were a genuine and authentic work of St. Luke, the companion of St. Paul, we have a fair picture of the man who was to become the apostle of Jesus Christ to the gentiles. There are some inconsistencies between the biographical references in The Acts and the Epistles, but these may be explained as resulting from misinformation or lapses of memory. They do not affect the essential elements of the account.

From his parents, the apostle received the name of Saul, and he was known as Saul of Tarsus until the time of his conversion. Though born in a gentile city, he was "a Hebrew of the Hebrews," and his father was a Pharisee of the tribes of Benjamin. Saul was

a citizen of Rome and was proud of this franchise. On
one occasion, the apostle was to be examined by scourg-
ing because of the complaints of the people of Jerusalem. The details are preserved in The Acts, 22: 25-29:
"And as they bound him with thongs, Paul said unto the
centurion that stood by, Is it lawful for you to scourge
a man that is a Roman, and uncondemned? When the
centurion heard that, he went and told the chief captain,
saying, Take heed what thou doest: for this man is a
Roman. Then the chief captain came, and said unto
him, Tell me, art thou a Roman? He said, Yea. And
the chief captain answered, With a great sum obtained
I this freedom. And Paul said, But I was free born.
Then straightway they departed from him which should
have examined him: and the chief captain also was
afraid, after he knew that he was a Roman, and because
he had bound him."

It would seem that Saul was of a substantial family,
and learned the Greek language in his youth. He also
had the trade of a tentmaker, but this does not indicate
the social level of his family. It was a custom among
all the Jews that every child, regardless of his estate,
should be taught a trade. Saul came to live in the city
of Jerusalem while still a youth. It is likely that he
settled in the Holy City in order to complete his education in the law of his fathers. Here he came under the
influence of Gamaliel, a celebrated doctor of the law,
whose advice to the Sanhedrin respecting the treatment
of the followers of Jesus is found in The Acts, 5: 38, 39:
"And now I say unto you, Refrain from these men, and
let them alone: for if this counsel or this work be of men,
it will come to nought: But if it be of God, ye cannot
overthrow it; lest haply ye be found even to fight
against God."

Gamaliel is mentioned as the first upon whom the title *rabban* was bestowed. He was president of the Sanhedrin during the reigns of Tiberius, Caligula, and Claudius, and was the grandson of Rabbi Hillel, a great teacher, who taught and practiced charity, humility, patience, and piety. Many of the sayings ascribed to him closely resemble the teachings of Jesus; for example: "What is unpleasant to thyself that do not to thy neighbor; this is the whole Law, all else is but its exposition." It is possible that through contact with Gamaliel young Saul was introduced to Jewish mysticism and to those concepts of religious conduct which dominated his life after he was converted.

Saul did not immediately accept the gentle and moderate advice of Gamaliel, but became one of those who persecuted the followers of Jesus. He may have disputed with Stephen, who was the chief of the seven deacons appointed to settle the complaint which had arisen between the Greek and Hebrew Christians. Stephen was executed by stoning outside the gates of Jerusalem, and was the first martyr of the faith. Saul was present at the stoning of Stephen, "consenting unto his death." In The Acts, 8: 3, Saul emerges as a violent adversary of the Christian community: "He made havoc of the church, entering into every house, and haling men and women committed them to prison." It was Saul's determination to destroy the new sect that caused him to make his celebrated journey to Damascus.

As Saul and his companions came near to Damascus, a light from heaven shone round about him, which blinded him even though it was midday. Saul fell to the earth, and a voice spoke to him from the light saying: "Saul, Saul, why persecutest thou me?" Of the conversion of Saul, Dr. William Smith writes: "That the Lord Jesus manifested Himself as a Living Person to the man Saul, and spoke to him so that his very words could be understood, is the substantial fact declared to us. The purport of the three narratives is that an actual conversation took place between Saul and the Lord Jesus. It is remarkable that in none of them is Saul said to have *seen* Jesus. . . . Externally there was a flash of light. Spiritually 'the light of the gospel of the glory of the Christ, who is the image of God,' shone upon Saul, and convicted the darkness of the heart which had shut out Love and knew not the glory of the Cross. Externally Saul fell to the ground. Spiritually he was prostrated by shame, when he knew whom he had been persecuting. Spiritually the Crucified said to Saul, with tender remonstrance, 'I am Jesus, why persecutest thou me?' Whether audibly to his companions, or audibly to the Lord Jesus only, Saul confessed himself in the spirit the servant of Him whose name he had hated. He gave himself up, without being able to see his way, to the disposal of him whom he now knew to have vindicated his claim over him by the very sacrifice which formerly he had despised. The Pharisee was converted, once and for all, into a disciple of Jesus the Crucified."

The thirteenth chapter of The Acts contains a reference to Saul in the first and seventh verses. The ninth verse reads: "Then Saul, (who also is called Paul,) filled with the Holy Ghost, set his eyes on him. . . ." The Bible supplies no further details as to this change of names, but it is generally accepted that the apostle took the name of Paul, which means *the small* (perhaps in the sense of *the lesser*) after he had accepted the Christian faith. The rest of the life and ministry of the apostle is familiar to all Bible students. He was as untiring in his devotion to his mission as previously he had been relentless in his persecution. Like many converts, he was more zealous than those with longer experience in the doctrine. Because of his scholarly attainments and his knowledge of the Greek language, it was natural that he should preach in Athens.

It was Paul who made possible the expansion of the Christian faith in a world of cultured and educated pagans. Some theologians have regarded his writings as strange and obscure, but to the learned of his own time he spoke a language which they understood. He may have been initiated into one of the mystical Fraternities which flourished in the regions where he lived or traveled. In I. Corinthians, 3:10, Paul writes: "According to the Grace of God which is given unto me, as a wise masterbuilder, I have laid the foundation, and another buildeth thereon. But let every man take heed how he buildeth thereupon." This seems to be a direct reference to the esoteric building Fraternities of Tyre and Sidon. St. Paul also "had a vow," and therefore had "shorn his head in Cenchrea." (See The Acts, 18:18.) These are only intimations, but they are more than sustained by the text of the writings attributed to him.

The important fact that Paul had never seen Jesus in the flesh not only divided him from the disciples, but also, in a way, separated him from the personality of Jesus. He was converted by a mystical experience within himself and not by long association with the Master. It is strange and wonderful that it should be Paul, who had never known Jesus the man, who alone understood the mystery of the Christ. That he did understand, we know from his words: "If any man is in

Christ he is a new creation." We cannot read the words
of Paul without realizing that the Christ whom he
preached was not the Jesus of the Gospels but the
Christos, the Anointed One, who was associated with
Jesus at the time of the baptizing by John. For the years
of the ministry, the Son of God and the son of man were
united in one appearance, but at the time of the crucifixion they separated again. In spite of the specific
teachings of Jesus, the disciples were not aware of the
qualitative difference between a personal redeemer and
a universal Saviour. It was the ministry of Paul which
rescued the Christian faith from the limitations of time
and locality. He made possible a universal faith universally demonstrable. Had this not occurred, we
should worship the history and not the mystery of Jesus.

Paul unfolded the Messianic tradition of the orthodox Jews by applying to it the Greek key to the mystery
of the Logos. God is one eternal principle containing
within itself all attributes and potencies. As eternal
life, Deity subsists forever in its own substance. As
Creator, Divinity manifests three qualities, or conditions. By the will of God, all things are fashioned; by
the love of God, all things are perfected; by the strength
of God, all things are sustained. Theologians have
defined Deity as one being in three persons. The divine
will is God the Father; the divine love is God the Son;
the divine strength is God the Holy Spirit, or the Comforter. The will of God is manifested as universal law,
which is both substantial and fruitful, sustaining the
generations of the living. The love of God is also both
substantial and fruitful, for it exists both in itself and
in those who have received it into their souls as a power
of spiritual generation. The strength of God is likewise
both substantial and fruitful, for it sustains all things

which come from the divine will, and, revealing itself
through mankind as the energy of faith, it multiplies
according to its kind.

The mystic experiences both the substance and the
fruitfulness of God intuitively or inwardly and bears
witness to the perfect working of the law through works
of godliness. The eternal Father is not here or there,
nor is he then or now, but an everlastingness—an ultimate of time and place in eternity. As the power of
God is forever, so likewise are his love and his strength.
All true wisdom is wisdom of God in God; all true love
and strength are likewise in God and of God. It is said
that the love of God endureth forever, and it is this love
which bears witness. In mortal matters, those whom
we love, we serve and cherish and preserve. How much
more, then, shall the perfect love of God serve and nourish and preserve his own? Is not also the divine love the
first born of the divine will? Does it not bear witness
before all nations, and is it not predestined and foreordained that in the presence of this love every knee
shall bend and acknowledge the universal Redeemer?

As the will of God brought forth the world-form as
a habitation for itself, so the love of God drew from the
deep the substances of the world-soul and entered into
this soul for the salvation of mankind. This is the incarnation described by Plato, when he said that the
Logos, in the infinite beginning, impressed itself upon
the substance of creation in the form of the cross. The
love of God embodied in the soul of creation is the universal Christos, the desired of all nations. Love is not
merely a human emotion; it is the manifestation of a
divine quality which has ensouled the subtler parts of
matter and fashioned them into an invisible habitation
for itself. The martyred Deity of the old pre-Christian

religions is this love of God, or God of love, slain for
the sin of the world.

Paul seems to have known this and to have realized
that only when Christ in a mystery is taught and understood can all sects and creeds be united on the level
of soul-insight, making possible one Shepherd and one
sheepfold. Men of different beliefs may accept or reject
the divinity of Jesus, but no one who has experienced
in his own heart the love of God can reject that love,
whether it be called the Christos or be known under
some other name. Paul sought to glorify the substance
and not the shadow, the message and not the messenger,
that witnessed and not that witnessing. His conversion
on the road to Damascus was his acceptance of the love
of God. Thereafter he wrote of it unceasingly and
preached it in Europe and Asia. He honored Jesus as
an embodiment or revealer of the Divine, who was
Christened when the love of the Father descended into
him in the waters of Jordan. To Paul, this was not only
a wondrous manifestation of the divine presence, but
a testimony and a covenant. By the mystery of the
proximity and availability of the divine love, all men
could know the truth, and the truth would set them free.

Although the Christian mystic uses the title *Christ*
as his name for the redeeming energy of God, this does
not imply religious or sectarian allegiance in the accepted meaning of such affiliation. There is no implication that the divine benevolence is available only to
those of a certain creed or nation or race. Consciousness
itself releases the heart and mind from concepts of
exclusiveness or superiority or preference. The fact
of the love of God is nameless, but for simple conveni-
ence it must be given some familiar designation. Other
great religious teachers have chosen terms from their

own languages and systems to imply the same wonderful truth. It is this truth, and not the name, which comforts the spirit.

The natural mysticism of the Christian religion was obscured by the theological controversies which disfigured the early centuries of the faith. Many prominent clerics solemnly declared that morality and good works were not acceptable to God as a means of salvation. Only complete conformity with the code of the approved sect was acceptable to Deity; otherwise virtuous conduct was a mortal sin. This attitude was approved by the Diet of Worms and reiterated in the Westminster Confession of Faith. With repentance more important than integrity, there was little emphasis upon the improvement of human character. Required to obey without question the solemn pronouncements of the clergy, the members of the congregation became wholly dependent upon absolution for their spiritual security.

How different was the spirit of the old prophets. Micah says: "Will the Lord be pleased with thousands of rams, or with ten thousand of rivers of oil? shall I give my firstborn for my transgression, the fruit of my body for the sin of my soul? He hath shewed thee, O man, what is good; and what doth the Lord require of thee, but to do justly, and to love mercy, and to walk humbly with thy God?" (Chap. 6:7, 8.) Many early mystics believed that Deity had implanted within the soul of man certain principles which manifest through intuition and instinct. We share a common impulse which impels us to kindliness, unselfishness, and faith. We are inclined to act in accordance with the moral potencies of our characters. It is only when we have been artificially conditioned by selfish and unreasonable doctrines that we are content to live badly.

Plato, who derived much of his philosophical system from Pythagoras, explained that God first produced the soul which is older than, and superior to, the body. The soul was made to command the body, and the body was made to obey the soul. By the wonderful processes of growth constantly operating in Nature, the world-body is being refined and regenerated and raised to a state of union with the world-soul. By analogy, the boay of man, derived from the substances of Nature, is subject to laws of regeneration and is gradually being transformed by the indwelling power of the soul. The body, therefore, fulfills its proper purpose by becoming responsive to the impulses of the soul by obeying them and fulfilling their requirements.

The Essenes were convinced that if they dwelt together keeping the law of the spirit they would receive a manifestation or revelation of the divine will. Through personal purity, humility, and love, the members of the Fraternity sought to draw toward the earth the Holy Spirit of the Lord, the coming of which would be announced by Elias, the forerunner, who would bring about the resurrection of the dead. In the terms of mysticism, Elias is faith, which prepares the way for the consummation of the Messianic mystery. St. Paul was influenced, to some degree, by this concept, and it recurs many times in early inspired writings. The Seven Churches formed together the constellation of the seven stars, as described in The Revelation, 1:16. This Christian constellation was the New Jerusalem adorned as a bride. All the Utopias originated in the idea of the establishment of the godly community among men. This community, sanctified and dedicated, was the Bride of the Lamb and the handmaiden of the Lord.

Once we realize that the external world is forever impelling us to examine within ourselves for parallels and analogies, we are both comforted and enlightened. We know that the life within us can be explained by the life around us. Universal Nature and human nature are alike in quality, even though they are different in quantity. If we will become thoughtfully aware of the intimations and implications provided by our environment and apply internally that which we observe externally, we transmute learning so that it becomes understanding. In order to be thus receptive, observant, and thoughtful, we must be dedicated to the search for truth and ever ready to learn its lessons. The refinements which result from the practice of mysticism make us more sensitive to the presence of the divine plan. Believing God to be everywhere, we intuitively perceive the divine presence in all things. This presence is not only a fact but a force. The omnipotent and omnipresent Deity is forever revealing itself through the creative processes which bear witness to its proximity.

When the inner eye is opened, man dwells forever in the presence of the Creator. Symbols no longer obscure the light of truth, but reveal it more abundantly. Death disappears in life, and darkness vanishes in light. God is no longer a distant and detached sovereignty ruling from a celestial throne. It is not necessary to accept the interpretations of theologians or to debate the articles of a creed. The will of God can be experienced, and the love of God can be known through direct acceptance by the faculties of the soul. Between the human being and this state of spiritual clarity are the frailties of his own flesh. Today when men attempt to practice internal quietude and solemnity, the silence is disturbed by an insistent worldliness which is, indeed, the thorn in the flesh. The mind conjures into existence a multitude of conflicting thoughts, and the emotions draw forth strange and contrary spirits from their own depths. We live in the midst of a mortal storm, and when we cry to the waves that they be still we cannot work the miracle.

Faith must prepare the way by cleansing our hearts and minds and relaxing the restlessness of the body. As faith grows within us, we develop a positive and substantial quietude. It is no longer an empty silence waiting to be filled, but a wise and loving peace already full of gratitude and gentle wonder. We can never know the truth about ourselves or our universe as long as we are dominated by our own opinions, prejudices, and conclusions. Even if these seem very wise and almost sufficient, we can never know their true worth until we have unfolded the divine plan in and through ourselves. This wonderful certitude impelled the early Christian communities to reject the entire structure of physical knowledge. They were wrong in so doing, because the works of man also reveal the way of heaven. Even today religion divides itself from other departments of human research. The soul rejects nothing, but by its own insight recognizes the divine plan.

To Paul, religion was not an institution or a philosophy. He had not found the consolation of the spirit through frequenting places of worship or by reading the learned writings of the illustrious teachers. Paul had passed from faithlessness to faith in an instant. This instant had no historical boundaries, no relationship to time or place. If this could happen to him, a sinner and a persecutor of the faithful, it could happen to others any time, anywhere. The miracle of the soul's awakening was by the grace of Christ as the interme-

diator between God and man. Some of the Church
Fathers taught that it was God working mysteriously
in the human heart that accomplished the wonder of
redemption. Others believed that it was man's own
earnest and dedicated effort which made possible the
union of human and divine consciousness. Paul was
a moderate force between historical and spiritualistic
religion. Most of all, however, he was moved by the
incident of his own conversion. Saul, a sinner, a corrupt
and evil man, a cynic and unbeliever, had been called
out of darkness to minister in the name of Jesus the
Christ. If this could happen, then, indeed, with God
all things are possible.

The infinite possibility of godliness made it most
urgent that all men should share in this hope and should
know that they live in the presence of a God who works
in mysterious ways. Many things Paul could not explain,
and least of all could he justify what had occurred to
himself. He was a new man in Christ, and with this
newness came a strong and abiding faith in the power
that had transformed him. He lived only to obey those
instincts which he believed originated in God's will.
If, then, all mankind could practice these same instincts,
might they not be accepted into the kingdom and
receive the blessed vision of the good life? Paul did
not substitute Christ for God, but considered the Saviour
as participating substantially in God. It is written in
the Torah that no man can see God and live, but that
which cannot be known factually can be experienced in
Christ, who bears witness to the Father. To receive
Christ as the spirit of grace is to know God, and to
reject Christ as the spirit of grace is to reject God.

Paul knew Christ as a patient voice speaking from
a great radiance. It was the effect of this voice upon

the soul of a human being that became the measure of the divine power. The effect could not be explained any more than could the cause which produced it. It was all a wonder, bearing witness to infinite love and understanding. The spirit of this wonder is Pauline Christianity. There are many miracles, but the greatest of these is Christ's love working through the hearts of men. When we perform the labors of the spirit, we reveal the substance of both fact and faith. Out of the radiance of our own consecration, the voice of the Master speaks to those whom we serve and cherish. The time for the good deed is always now; this can be the moment of the revelation. To pause in the works of good for signs and omens and seasons is to deny the immediate realization of the divine will.

While men struggle to perfect a way of life, building monuments to their own confusion, and growing by the long, tired path of pain, the teachings of Paul are worth immediate attention. The solution to problems is no further from us than our own capacity to fulfill the dictates of the soul in our heart. Even as we ask for answers to our worldly dilemmas, we know these answers and have always known them, but we have lacked the courage to keep the spirit of our code. The simple act of faith courageously performed makes available to each of us the ageless wisdom which is within us.

Although very little is known about the early development of Christianity, the mysticism of St. Paul and the mystical theology of St. John exerted a strong influence from the beginning. The *Pastor* of Hermas and the writings of St. Perpetua, Tertullian, and especially Clement of Alexandria include numerous references to religious raptures, ecstasies, and revelations by the spirit. Clement, in his effort to discredit the Gnostics, made several comparisons of Christian and pagan mystical disciplines intended to prove that the followers of Christ practiced a way of contemplation by which they were able to understand the mysteries of the spirit by divine grace. Origen distinguished two kinds of living, which he called *active* and *contemplative*. He was dedicated to a life of asceticism, and his example was followed by St. Anthony.

Considered formally, mysticism is based upon four interrelated concepts that are to be found among all religious groups which emphasize illumination from within the nature:

1. The existence of a technique for the strengthening and perfecting of internal metaphysical powers and faculties.
2. The cultivation of quietism, or the suspension of the activities of the objective mental and emotional functions of the personality.
3. The use of introspection, or the turning inward of the focus of awareness, accompanied by a release from all opinions and attitudes previously held or admired.
4. A disregard for, or renunciation of, worldly honors or such responsibilities as may result from attachments to physical things and material institutions.

Although the theological aspect of Christianity received the larger share of attention, mysticism is strongly sustained by the conduct of Christ in the various stages of his ministry. The transfiguration of Jesus, as described in Matt. 17:2, is characteristic of the genuine mystical experience. In the great decision which marked the termination of his earthly career, the Master was guided completely by what has been called an interior sense of life. In him, the two spheres of substance and shadow were united beyond conflict. These spheres correspond to the contemplative and active lives described by Origen. Jesus attuned his mortal nature so perfectly with the Beyond, or source of being, that he was able to sustain the son-Father experience of consciousness even when he was hanging upon the cross.

Though St. Paul intimates that mystical unfoldment through divine infolding is possible through a series of unitive steps or stages, mysticism, as it has developed in Western religion, is felt or known rather than rationalized. Normal human life is marked by a dual focus of awareness known as the subject-object state. When consciousness is directed toward subject it is called subjective, and when directed toward object it is called objective. Usually, little effort is made to bridge or unify these states. We have an inner life which we may consider sacred and private, and an outer life which we accept as profane and public.

Ethics has to do with the application of subject principles to object occurrences. To a degree, therefore, our outer lives affect our inner convictions, and vice versa. The more we live from within, the more idealistic our policies; whereas, the more we are focused upon externals, the more materialistic our codes of conduct. The sense of selfhood is poised between the two spheres or states. By direct action of the will, it may verge toward one or the other, which it can do only because it accepts the existence of each of these levels as a separate reality.

This is the danger which first presents itself to the truth seeker. Even though he dedicates his energies to the quest for reality, he approaches Being as a spectator rather than as a participant. In the end he becomes a theologian and not a mystic. He may discover many wonderful facts about the workings of the divine power. These facts may possess him, and such possession brings with it a sense of exaltation rather than a realization of intimacy. The scientist of the future may be able to penetrate the intangible wall which divides subject and object, but as long as he remains addicted to the scientific focus of discernment, the words of Sir Edward Arnold will remain applicable: "Veil upon veil he lifts to find veil upon veil behind."

In the Christian mystery, there is not only the factor of human aspiration, but also a direct outpouring of transcendant energy from the subject or life-source. This is accompanied by a complete shattering of the subject-object concept within ourselves. The center of soul-awareness in man experiences a state of identity in which there are no images, ideas, attitudes, or symbols derived from the objective, or outer, level of living. This has been described as the journey of the alone to the Alone. To clarify definitions which inevitably must be inadequate, we may say that the mystic has released himself or has been released by the divine power from the acceptance of a universe existing in two states. This release comes in the form of an irresistible surge of life from Being itself. This surge is accompanied by an indescribable awareness of the presence of the Divine. Such awareness requires neither explanation nor justification. It cannot be differentiated by the mind or the emotions and is marked by a peculiar intense enthusiasm (*entheos*, meaning *in God*).

We cannot too strongly emphasize the liberation of the soul from the subject-object hypnosis. It is in the interval between what we believe to be subject and object that our uncertainties grow and flourish. We are suspended between opposites, which obviously are irreconcilable while they remain apart. Conscience is a simple instance of conflict between principle and practice or between code and conduct.

The Christian mystics, both Catholic and Protestant, were still troubled by the duality of the contemplative and active levels on which the human being functions. They instinctively cultivated the contemplative level because it seemed to lead away from involvement in those mortal concerns which most impede the pilgrim's progress. The result was the rise of asceticism and the elevation of the solitary life as superior in godliness to the active life.

Modern truth seekers frequently fall into this dilemma. They belittle their human responsibilities and depreciate the achievements of others, fondly believing that by so doing they enlarge in spiritual stature. All they actually prove is that they are afraid of the object state and lack the courage to apply their ideals in an uncongenial environment. They may lift themselves to a better ethical level by the practice of self-control, but they have not corrected the cause of personal inharmony.

As a psychological phenomenon, the mystical experience seems to be the subjective discovery of the wholeness of the self. No other explanation so completely defines the mystery. The human being is a complex of separate and distinct impulses arising from highly diversified centers of function and faculty. Nearly always we know ourselves in terms of parts. Sometimes we are astonished and dismayed at phases of our own disposition and temperament which emerge under pressures. The acceptance of our divided power-resources not only weakens our faith in ourselves, but opens us to countless conflicts and disturbances. When in a state of spiritual exaltation, the soul is felt as an entirety rather than as

an entity. Being envelops beings, and the single purpose
of life ensouls and possesses all those attributes which
have previously functioned as separate focal points of
energy.

St. Paul's interpretation of Christ can be understood
as the perfect example of the union of subject and
object. Christ as subject possessed completely Jesus as
object. The two were thus wholly one and supplied the
perfect pattern or witness of the Christened state. By
extension, this mystery foreshadows the ultimate relationship between God as eternal subject and mankind
as natural object. The Christ-Jesus relationship fore-
shadowed the God-man relationship, thus providing the
eternal hope or promise.

The Christian mystic experiences the inflow of Being
by a series of reflexes and acceptances. These together
emerge in the substantial subjective likeness of Christ.
Thus Christ is the whole self and the whole being. Even
though the influx of the consciousness of God may be
accompanied by extreme agitation, the mental and emotional responses are on the level of sublimity. We are
moved by an inevitable tenderness, and react as though
purified and cleansed of weakness and insufficiency.
The incredible beauty, combined with a wondrous
strength, is intuitively accepted as a divine presence,
We clothe this presence in the most radiant and perfect
form that religion has given, which is the redeeming
power of the Saviour. Redemption is explained as a
process of being made whole. We interpret this usually
as the recovery of the body from some indisposition, but
when Jesus taught that faith bestows wholeness, he
spoke as a mystic and a physician of the soul.

While St. Paul used only the terms available in his
time, he was certainly aware of the subject-object se-

quence. The Christ-Jesus identity came to him as a greater mystery than the world had ever known. The immortal-mortal was now a fact and the source of a new dispensation or way of life for humanity. Paul was no longer an individual. He personified collective mankind, but not in the same way that Jesus had previously embodied the human potential. Jesus was the one who succeeded, and Paul was the one who must not fail. Through the union of Christ and Jesus, a condition had been established in the spiritual fact of living. Paul received this condition and preached Jesus, the Christened. The substance of subject and object confirmed in the divine mystery bestowed a new dimension or quality on the level of soul power. Christendom tried to explain this by emphasizing the uniqueness of its ministry, but based its claim upon historical, rather than mystical, truths.

There are references to the cosmic import of the Christ event, but without the mystical experience it is not possible to apperceive in consciousness the meaning of the Lamb of God that was slain for the sin of the world. Paul seems to have known, but could not convey to others that which he knew except by his constant injunction to practice the internal Christ. No longer was redemption to descend, like the light of the sun, from the great source of power. Salvation must be released through those creatures in which and for which it had given its life. The seed had been quickened and could be known and experienced. Those seeds which fell on good ground increased a hundredfold. Paul was not boasting when he said that he was an apostle of Christ-Jesus. He was telling a story to a world that did not understand and which does not yet understand.

THE MYSTICAL EXPERIENCE
Engraving by Albrecht Durer

Chapter Ten

CHRIST IN YOU, THE HOPE OF GLORY

In the course of years, countless problems of human living have been brought to my attention. Kindly, well-intentioned men and women have come to me with their hopes, their fears, their sorrows, and their grievances. For most of us, living is a confusion of fortune and misfortune, of hopes unfulfilled, and loves unrequited. We wonder why a beautiful earth, so abundantly supplied with everything necessary for peace and security, should be so mutilated by human conduct. Even while we are perturbed by the conflict of nations, we examine our personal environments and find them also discordant. Everywhere there is unrest and a desperate striving. We stand ever ready to sacrifice ourselves and all that we have to advance causes devoid of essential merit.

In this uneasy generation, few achieve even a semblance of personal contentment. We are assured that if we pause to enjoy the experience of living, we are false to a code that requires us to hasten on until at last we dash headlong into an open grave. We live daily fearing our neighbors, and certain that others lie in wait to steal our goods. Crime is increasing, and sickness caused by tension and stress afflicts both the successful and the unsuccessful. Those who have are servants to their goods, and those who have not are in bondage to their ideologies. Ever ready to die for something, we seem unable to live for anything.

Yet in the midst of the prevailing demoralization stands the unchanging human being. He is the embodiment of good intentions and, no matter how badly he lives, affirms his addiction to high principles. He beholds himself as the eternal victim of conditions beyond his control. He seldom analyzes these so-called conditions, and accepts no responsibility for his part in the fashioning of them. He declines to consider that he is a factor in someone else's pattern of experience. To all but ourselves, each of us is part of the collective pressure which burdens mortal existence.

Why are we such negative units in that mass which we call humanity? How does it happen that more than two billion men and women, most of them essentially good-natured and kind-hearted, can so corrupt the laws of God, Nature, and man as to exist in a condition of perpetual anxiety? Do the tragedies we suffer from descend upon us from heaven, ascend from the earth, or emerge from ourselves? Thoughtfulness sustains the last possibility. We have been given the power and ability to build a proper way of life, but some perverse spirit seems to corrupt our instincts. It is easy to shift responsibility and insist that strong and evil men conspire against our security for their own advantage. We excuse our own misdeeds by blaming bad laws, corrupt politicians, or benighted theologians. These evasions, however, solve nothing, and each day we face the future with more numerous misgivings.

It is not always wise or fair to generalize upon particulars, but those in certain departments of public life have better opportunities to observe the conduct of their fellow men than is given to the average person. Slowly but surely a mass of evidence accumulates which indicates prevailing tendencies and practices. The findings of individuals can be checked with specialists in the field, who have gathered data from all brackets of society. Such testimony cannot be denied and should not be ignored. The human personality is not so mysterious that it cannot be analyzed, nor is the average individual so unique that his reactions violate the pattern of expectancy. Even when we try to be different, we are surprisingly similar.

The most common of all personality phenomena is the inability to resist impulse. We can defend ourselves from all persuasions except our own. The moment we feel an urge toward an attitude or an action, we are helpless. We not only lack the strength to oppose our personal desires, but also the inclination. Whatever the feeling may be, no matter how unreasonable or destructive, we can be restrained only by fear of physical consequences. Even these may not deter us unless they are accompanied by heavy penalties enforced by law. The complete absence of self-censorship or, as it is often called, self-control in the conduct of our private affairs often leads to tragedy. When we add to this the mental habits which permit us to exonerate ourselves from all moral responsibility for our own misdeeds, our constitutions are at the mercy of our whims.

Moral education is largely concerned with the refining of our natural instincts. We cannot control the human being by imposing upon him an ethical code which is contrary to his inclinations. It is first necessary to civilize these inclinations and redirect the energies which they release. It has been my observation, after more than thirty years direct contact with groups and individuals, that the average person's philosophy of life resolves itself into the formula: "I *must* do exactly what I *want* to do." *Must*, in this case, means an irresistible compulsion justified by basic desire. When you suggest that perhaps it would be possible to modify the determination, the usual answer is: "I can't." Thus in two words we are told that there are no means or facilities which can restrain a blind urge. Where the urge comes from and what the consequences will be are of no concern.

Later, if impulse results in a miserable situation, there may be moments of repentance. We wish we had not permitted ourselves to commit a foolish action, but the next day we repeat the mistake, thereby proving that it is quite possible not to learn from experience. Many ingenious defense mechanisms support our inclinations. We can conveniently forget what we have done even though our memories are so retentive that we never forget what others have done to us. With similar enthusiasm, we can deny flatly and emphatically recent words or actions. We cannot hope to be believed by others, but we are trying desperately to convince ourselves. All other means of evasion failing, we adamantly refuse to consider the subject any further. It might sound as though such habits would make us disagreeable. In extreme cases this is true, but, for the most part, we are just pleasant people with unpleasant peculiarities.

Even though our moral codes are numerous, personal morality has not reached an advanced stage of development. We do not actually believe in the utility of the standards which we are pledged to maintain. Integrity is desirable in others and indispensable in those with whom we have relationship, but it is not the most important ingredient in our own compound. Deeper and older than the proprieties is dedication to self-satisfaction. If we can keep the law and do as we please, so much the better; otherwise, we shall do as we please. There is the further comforting thought that we are just one person out of the multitude, and our own habits and practices cannot greatly influence the destiny of civilization. We do not realize that millions of others feel the same way, and after their common policy comes the deluge. We proceed through life refusing to accept responsibility for ourselves, far more interested in fulfilling our instincts than keeping faith with the universe and its rules.

It is inevitable that those practicing the "I can't help it" program should ultimately find themselves in embarrassing situations. They have violated the common law even though they may not have broken a legal code. Having lost their friends, broken their homes, estranged their children, and squandered their means, they seek help and advice. Even this perfectly sincere action does not imply that there is any intention to correct the basic cause of the unhappiness. Even while they explain their troubles, these sufferers defend the very attitudes which caused the trouble. The advice that is given is seldom applied if it is contrary to inclination, and any suggestion that would be helpful will most certainly be unpopular. Having endorsed the corrective program and with solemn assurance that it shall be kept to the letter, the miserable mortal goes forth and does exactly what he did before because he "can't help it."

It is observable that negative instincts are most frequently found and most dangerously exercised by those who have little or no religious consciousness. This does not mean that they are not nominally addicted to theology. They may belong to one or more of the numerous denominations, orthodox or unorthodox, which flourish today. They may be regular churchgoers or follow independent religious educators. They may even be enthusiastic devotees devoting their lives to religious or philosophical subjects. At the same time they are substantially untouched internally by the implications of a spiritual tradition. Their beliefs have never penetrated into the zone of instincts and therefore have not modified or refined the pressures which impel conduct. No matter what we believe, we have not found the consolation of a faith while we still permit ourselves to practice negative procedures because we "can't help it." The purpose of religion is to equip us to say: "I can control myself."

The modern tendency in religion is to drift with the dominant motions of society. The churches depend upon public support, and therefore must cater to the collective whim. The intangibles are the first to be sacrificed. These idealistic overtones place certain requirements upon character. In the practice of his religion, a church member in good standing is expected to contribute financially to the maintenance of the sect and to contribute ethically to the maintenance of society. The latter responsibility is largely ignored, with the result that ethical and moral levels are not maintained. It is easy to blame our institutions for their failure to enforce their principles, but it is impossible for groups depending upon public support to proceed contrary to the policies of their members and still survive.

Religious teachings are useful only to the degree that they enrich the internal lives of human beings. This enrichment takes many forms, but always 'it strengthens the resolution to preserve the spiritual wealth and the cultural heritage of the race. From the fountains of our faith have flowed art, music, literature, science, and philosophy. All that is beautiful, noble, and inspired is sustained by consciousness, which chooses to give of its worldly possessions in order that it may preserve and protect the great intangibles. Collective experience has justified this concept of values, and we know that we live in a better world because a very small minority of idealists has kept faith with convictions of consciousness and has recognized the sustaining power of illumined integrity. These idealists accomplished what their contemporaries solemnly declared to be impossible, because they refused to compromise their principles. The lives of these heroes include numerous accounts of the struggle against internal weakness. There were frequent opportunities and inducements to compromise the resolution of the spirit. Achievement was not because of public support, but in spite of popular opposition.

What inspired leaders are to collective society, noble convictions are to the individual. Without these, all of his other activities are without lasting merit. As we have persecuted the prophets of the world, so we frustrate our own impulses which would impel us to self-improvement. When vision fails in society, the nation perishes, and when it fails in us, we cease to fulfill our natural destiny. The evidence of ethical decline is personality insecurity. To the degree that we depart from principles, we separate ourselves from the source of life and growth. Like the leaf that has fallen from the tree, we no longer receive into ourselves the life-giving energies of the universal parent. If thus separated, we are doomed to failure even though we appear to succeed and to accumulate for ourselves a large share of the treasures of the earth.

Regardless of the number and quality of our acquisitions, we must all live with ourselves. If this relationship becomes intolerable for any reason, the possessions for which we have sacrificed character bestow neither comfort nor contentment. Those who are without faith, hope, and love are in bankruptcy, and depend for their internal survival upon the kindness and unselfishness of others. We know that it is not easy to sacrifice things imminently desirable in order to attain other things eminently necessary. There is the further implication that we constantly experience the external life, and have grown shrewd in estimating its material values. We do not wish to look forward to moderate living when, by sharp practice, there is a probability of opulence. Integrity does not appear profitable in terms of physical advantage. As one person said to me: "The wise are usually poor, the virtuous misunderstood, humanitarians ridiculed, and the saints martyred." A world which respects false values and penalizes noble convictions offers slight inducement to those trying to decide upon a future course of action.

Available clinical data strongly supports the importance of a mature personal philosophy for living.

Those who have religious and ethical foundations meet critical situations with less damage to themselves and others. Many persons, however, are not able to find inspiration and consolation in the creeds of their ancestors. The need for religious inspiration remains, but the means for satisfying this instinct are not soulsufficient. The immediate solution is mysticism, which invites the individual to seek his living values from within himself. The very thoughtfulness which impels us to supply a recognized deficiency of character provides a means for accomplishing the desired end. The moment we realize the source of the weakness of our conduct, we intuitively know what we must do.

This knowledge and the implications which it forces upon our attention nearly always impel censorship over conduct. We become acutely aware that we are contributing constantly to our own misfortunes. We cannot improve the state in which we exist without changing the quality of our thoughts and emotions. As long as we continue on the present level of motivation, we must endure the problems peculiar to that level. It is one thing to accept this fact intellectually, and quite another to experience it as a conviction of consciousness. The acceptance is static, but the conviction is dynamic. Fortunately, we possess internal faculties which make possible an apperception of truth as it relates to our own needs.

Christian mysticism is the solution to the immediate problems of Christendom. As long as Christian nations dominate world policies, they also exercise a powerful influence upon all the social and political groups belonging to other faiths. The only way in which a dominant culture can unfold and flourish is to maintain both privately and publicly the principles and practices upon which that culture was founded. The life and teachings of Jesus not only exemplify the Christian way of life, but also provide a legal and moral code which cannot be violated without disastrous consequences. Many persons feel that the Christian code as taught by the Master is too advanced and too idealistic to be applicable under existing conditions. If this be true, the human race has not yet advanced beyond the state of barbarism and must bear the heavy burden of its own shortcomings. There is no escape from insufficiency except to become sufficient. It is not lack of ability, but lack of enlightened incentive that holds us back. A level of intellectual development which has made possible the atomic bomb and the Mt. Palomar telescope is capable of appreciating and understanding the Sermon on the Mount. If we are not bewildered by the wonders of the visible universe, there is no reason why we should consider our spiritual requirements to be incomprehensible.

While it may sound profane to speak of spiritual values in terms of dollars and cents, it brings the subject closer to persons whose minds are obsessed by the monetary system. Those seeking advice frequently preface their remarks by enumerating the sums they have already spent seeking relief from their disorders. The amounts vary with the financial status of the individual, and range from a few dollars to vast expenditures. Several persons have told me that they have impoverished themselves and burdened their children without finding adequate relief. It was evident that no amount of money could buy internal security for these persons. The fault lay within themselves, and only there could it be corrected. A large part of the money spent in this country on doctors, psychiatrists, and lawyers could be used to advance our culture, instead of being wasted on the repairing of broken lives, if we had a more mature standard of values.

As a people we lack dedication to cherished convictions. The Christian code is completely practical if we are willing to apply it and sacrifice selfish interests to its preservation. Occasionally, we find someone who has recognized the facts, has made his decision, and has kept it. We do not observe that this dedication has brought with it the disasters commonly expected. The person is happier, healthier, more popular, and more useful. The new life which he has experienced has brought with it so many benefits that he can only wonder why he lacked the courage to make the effort sooner. We often quote the familiar words: "Blessed is little and peace of mind," but we have strong reservations against that part which says: "Blessed is little." It is wise to remember that religion does not require that we renounce our worldly goods. Such a degree of detachment is impelled from within ourselves, and if or when such a resolution arises, it is not accompanied by a sense of loss but by a feeling of relief. We cannot give up anything we want, nor will we keep anything which we no longer desire.

If we have the instinct to preserve our grudges even though they destroy us, we should not find it difficult to make constructive decisions. It is a matter of impulses which must be wisely and lovingly educated. We expend a great deal of time and energy enriching the mind because we hope that its faculties will, in turn, provide security for the body. We are perfectly willing to inconvenience ourselves and practice uncongenial trades and professions through the best years of our lives in order to insure our creature comforts. We are sustained by the thought that the end justifies the means, but we are much less inclined to sacrifice our instincts to the preservation of the person who lives in the body.

No individual is a satisfactory human being until his outer activities serve generous and constructive internal convictions. Life without purpose is a burden to the end. When we are disturbed and disconsolate inwardly, we transfer our attention to material ambitions, which are only escape mechanisms. Modern civilization is a monument to human beings running away from themselves. The greater the pressure behind the escape mechanism, the more disagreeable and dangerous will be our physical careers. Tyrants, rogues, and despots are merely strong, unhappy persons, whose frustrations have caused an oversecretion of bile. This is the same bile which Samuel Johnson declared to be the principal cause of war.

We have been given a beautiful teaching to which the better parts of our own natures instinctively aspire. As never before, we need to live and understand the original Christian code. We must cleanse our minds of the tendency to associate the teachings of Jesus with the false concepts which have been circulated in his name. We may not be able to convert the unbelievers in far places, but we can strengthen the faith in our own hearts.

One person who came to me seeking spiritual consolation was a picture of piety. His remarks were well-larded with Scriptural quotations and punctuated with mountainous sighs. At times it seemed as though he had actually convinced himself that he was a paragon of Christian virtues. At the same time, this man was devoured by hate. He loved everyone in general, and hated everyone in particular. He had nursed grudges until he had wrecked his nervous system and poisoned his body. He neither forgave nor forgot, but could recount to the smallest detail every injustice which he fondly believed had been heaped upon him. In no part of his narration did he recognize any fault in himself. He must have been impossible to live with, for even an hour of his presence was most fatiguing. The natural kindness, which is an essential part of human nature, was entirely lacking in this man. He suffered, and retaliated by making others suffer; yet he would have been mortally insulted had it been suggested to him that he was not a fine Christian gentleman.

This embittered one may be an extreme example, but he was typical of an incredible inconsistency. He complained against an unprincipled world, yet was himself without principles. Certainly this man had never experienced the consolation of the spirit and had no inclination to do good to those who despitefully used him. Yet this simple and gentle doctrine was the only remedy for the sickness which possessed his soul. Unless he accepted it with the fullness of his heart, he would continue his unhappy course until death ended his mortal career. No amount of advice would be of any practical value. Other human beings could never cater sufficiently to his whims to bring him contentment. Even if he had his own way in everything, he would still be unhappy because his own way was wrong. To reason with such a person and to point out to him the falseness of his attitudes is to receive that all-embracing justification: "I can't help it." This particular man was as completely addicted to his ways as the alcoholic or the drug addict. He lived for his grievances and would perish without them. He enjoyed his characteristics, but resented their consequences. He wanted to be happy and at the same time cherish and protect the cause of unhappiness.

If it so happens that your life seems ineffective, burdensome, or afflicted, seek within your own heart and mind for the cause and the cure. We are a wonderfully privileged national group. Opportunities for self-improvement and self-expression are abundant if we will be satisfied with reasonable efforts. In a universe filled with things to know and work to do, we are bored and neurotic. More, today, suffer from lack of constructive activity than from overwork. The physical requirements of survival are being simplified, and this generation has leisure unknown to our ancestors. Freedom from responsibility, however, has not inspired effort, but has contributed to indolence.

Hundreds of persons have sought help from me because they had nothing to do and were without constructive interests. We interpret activity only in terms of material endeavor. The social life is devoid of significance, and even intelligent conversation is a lost art. We are reduced to superficial activities to fill time which would otherwise be devoted to self-pity or the criticism of each other. The simple pleasures and duties which occupied the lives of our forebears are no longer attractive. Having freed our hands from manual labor, we have left the mind without employment. This career of genteel vegetating has been turned over to the keeping of the imagination which builds a fool's paradise for ourselves and a purgatory for those around us.

Mysticism changes the complexion of daily existence. It enriches the internal life by giving it beauty and loftiness of perspective. Most of all it directs our attention upon the untutored self which lurks behind the mask of our sophistication. We experience the pressing need for a program that will occupy our hearts and minds as long as we live. If we will practice the Beatitudes, by knowing in our hearts that they are true and revealing this knowledge through our conduct, we will not need to frequent psychologists and domestic counselors. The mystic knows the dignity of those small incidents which we are inclined to regard as trifling. It was Michelangelo who said: "Trifles make perfection, but perfection is no trifle."

The human being is not naturally equipped for vast projects. He is happiest and best oriented when he enjoys the simple benefits of living and shares them with those whom he loves. He will find more peace in a garden than in a palace, more contentment in his own home than in some vast monument to his economic acumen. Inordinate ambitions have disfigured human society since men first sought greater worlds to conquer. We could all enjoy a rich and full life and preserve the health necessary for contentment if we substituted internal growth for economic expansion. We might have the expansion also, but it would be ensouled with an ethical policy sufficiently strong and idealistic to curb the abuses associated with our competitive economic psychology.

Spiritual integrity does not limit effort, but directs it, making it essentially significant in the plan of human progress. It is not back to religion, but forward to the application of faith to works. We have not outgrown spiritual convictions; we have simply moved past older interpretations and applications. We are not happy; therefore, we are not truly wise. We are not contented; therefore, we are not truly good. Further explanations simply complicate and obscure the facts. Devotion to the presence of God in our own soul is not superstition, nor does it imply a weakening of the mental powers. We are not better because we have freed ourselves from the false gods of the past. We are more intelligent when we dedicate ourselves to the eternal spirit which pervades all things whether or not we accept this fact.

All over the world simple people gather in prayer and devotion in the sanctuaries of their religions. Perhaps these devout believers have never made brilliant or brittle contributions to the sophistry of their time. Yet, with faults, failings, and limitations, they have kept the faith and have received a wonderful strength. In their homes they care for their families, and in all emergencies seek and find consolation in communion with their God. In small communities where the old ways survive, there are no locks on the doors, no alms-houses or jails. The people work side by side in the fields, and the children help as soon as they are able. Everyone is busy; and if sickness comes, the strong serve the weak and bring in the harvest. There is a wonderful integrity in those regions where the pressures of living have not reached. Perhaps it is accompanied by a lack of advantages, but it teaches a lesson to those who have eyes in their hearts.

It may well be that we live on a higher social level and enjoy numerous privileges unknown in less advanced communities, but progress does not justify loss of integrity. We are far better equipped to appreciate real values and support them. The composite picture obscures the human equation. As individuals we have not changed in our basic requirements because we have complicated our activities. Happiness must still be earned in the same old way. Peace and contentment still bless the grateful heart, and larger learning gives us a fuller opportunity to experience and share the wisdom of our love. The policies which dominated the Essenian community so long ago are still the most practical way of life. It can be on any plane of human function, but it must supply the pattern of integrity if the social order is to survive.

Each of us has a small environment over which we exercise a measure of authority. It is in this little world that we must begin to practice the teachings of Jesus. This does not mean that we must resign ourselves to some patient program of silent suffering. In the home, the office, and places of social gathering, we bring the benediction of understanding if we have found our faith. The more perfectly we exemplify our principles, the larger our sphere of influence will become. We shall be sought out by those who have sensed our inner security. Our conduct speaks more loudly and more authoritatively than our words, and we shall understand that truly the harvest is ready, but the laborers are few. When we have demonstrable answers to eternal questions, we shall never lack for things to do. There will be little time left, and each day will be rich in privileges. We are lonely because others do not need our complaints, but our positive contributions to courage and constructive thinking will be acceptable to many.

If we can convince ourselves that we are the most miserable of mortals, which is a false conviction at best, can we not also prove to our own satisfaction that we have the capacity to be useful and inspiring? Why not make a career of service rather than of complaint? Most will say that they would if they could. Let these know that they can, for within them is a source of life and supply which is sufficient to the demands of the occasion. Between that source and its perfect expression is imposed the complex structure of the human personality. While we continue to cater to the intemperances of this unregenerate psychological entity, we stand not only in our own light, but also in the way of a divine light which would otherwise shine into the lives of others. Selfishness not only deforms ourselves, but betrays the spirit of truth which is locked within us.

We are not naturally or instinctively a devotional people except in moments of tragedy. We are not grateful for our blessings, but quick to recognize our misfortunes. We must criticize less, and understand more if we are to solve the riddle of human destiny. It will profit us little to engage upon an elaborate program of religious research in an effort to determine which of the faiths of men is the nearest to the universal will. This would be our natural inclination because it would be consistent with those inconsistencies which dominate collective conduct. The way of light for us, regardless of our intellectual or cultural attainments, leads back into ourselves and through the innermost parts of our beings toward the eternal God. Until we make this journey, we must remain uncertain, depending upon the opinions of others for a knowledge which can be certified only by ourselves. Religions may be persecuted and various restrictions imposed upon the outer activities of peoples, but the road inward cannot be blocked by the despotism of mortals or the tyranny of time. Each individual, from the highest to the lowest, regardless of his means or his social estate, must make the same quiet journey. There is no other way, and the road can never be closed.

To the Christian mystic, the path of contemplation leads to the feet of Christ. It is consummated by the personal experience of the Saviour, who is known as a wonderful presence full of mercy and of grace. This presence calls to those who are weary and heavy-laden, bestowing rest. In moments of rapture, the aspiring human heart seems to touch the source of the world's love. In that instant, there is a glorious replenishing of faith and resolution. There is a courage which is not of this world, and we are able to face any emergency without fear or doubt. There are many who long after this soul-experience. They pray that it may be given to them and that they may be worthy to receive it, but even sincere prayer is not enough unless it strengthens the resolution to live the mystical discipline.

World leaders who are responsible for the future of their States stand in constant need of communion with the spirit. This can come to them only when, by a resolution of conscience, they have purified their hearts and minds of selfishness and corruption. Doctors become great physicians only when they dedicate their lives and their skill to the God within themselves. Judges and lawyers judge righteously and defend with honor when they follow the dictates and directions of heaven. Educators teach wisely only when they teach truly, and they cannot bestow truth until their minds and hearts have been possessed by the spirit of truth. Business men, craftsmen, and traders contribute to the improvement and security of others when in their hearts they keep faith. Fathers, mothers, husbands, wives, and children experience the true dignity of their human relationships, protecting each other, assisting each other, and fulfilling each other when enlightened love, which is unselfish, guides their decisions and inspires their conduct. Everywhere and always, we must move from the sacred center of our natures and not from the insistencies of egotism.

Those who scoff at the possibility of internal resources, who deny the very existence of a benign principle at the source of life, and who ridicule man's simple faith in the immortality of the human soul and the ultimate perfection of all living creatures will be properly offended. They will report that we have departed from all practical activities and given ourselves over to a sickly idealism sustained by illusion. It is easy for the ignorant to pass judgment upon the wise, but what have these critics to offer by way of personal example? Are they happy? Are their homes secure? Are they respected citizens, and do they live generous and useful lives? The very fact that they condemn others witnesses their own uneasiness. They resent qualities which they do not possess, and would impose their own insufficiencies upon a sorrowing world.

It has been my privilege to know many who were wise in their own conceits. Not one of them was any better for his unbelief. In freeing his mind from what he liked to believe to be the delusions of the underprivileged, he deprived himself also of natural peace of mind. Some of these self-emancipated molders of public opinion have confided to me, in those rare moments when they were honest with themselves, that they were miserable derelicts on the sea of life. They had nothing worth while to live for and could only hope that the grave was synonymous with oblivion. Such individuals live on the surface because they are afraid of depth. They do not dare to turn inward lest they be drowned in their own darkness.

Children growing up today need religious instruction, but even more they need enlightened example.

We cannot hope to maintain law and order in human society unless we provide an inspiring and inspired code. It is a mistake to say that children cannot be controlled. The young spend many long years passing through various degrees of hero-worship. Whatever is important to the adult is equally significant to the child. The natural idealism of the young is frustrated by the inconsistency everywhere revealed in the conduct of adults. The parents bestow moral platitudes upon their offspring, and at the same moment violate the very doctrines which they preach. The child gradually learns that there is no essential relationship between things said and actions performed. All child psychologists and those working with problems of juvenile delinquency emphasize that the lack of dignity, honor, and integrity in the home life is responsible for the present unhappy picture. Parents would find their children more comforting, especially in later years, if children found their parents more comforting, especially in earlier years.

Mysticism, by transforming the core of human attitudes, can prevent the tragedies which all too often cannot later be remedied. The failure of human nature to defend and maintain a high level of integrity underlies most of the news that is banner-headed in the local press. We read the morning paper and, for a moment at least, we are profoundly concerned. We say that times are bad, but they will remain bad until we learn the lesson and mend our own ways. We are inclined to accept the hereditary factor and to think it quite likely that our children inherit peculiarities of appearance and temperament. When we realize what these peculiarities have done to complicate our living, should we not hesitate to pass them on to our descendants?

The corrections which we make in ourselves and the improvements which we bestow upon our bodies through the attainments of our hearts and minds may well give a better heritage to those for whom we sacrifice in so many other ways. The greatest legacy that can be given to a child is the united love of its parents revealed through an orderly, constructive, and creative home environment. Can we provide this without first improving ourselves?

Internal strength is our strongest defense against the encroachments of negative pressures which are always an integral part of environment. We should build no walls against the lessons taught by experience; rather we should accept the lessons, realizing that they are opportunities for self-improvement. Instead of rebelling and locking our hearts and minds, we should seek a better standard of living through the enrichment of consciousness and the resolution to react constructively to the challenge of adversity. We may not feel that we have the strength or the resources to sustain personal integrity, and it is this realization of insufficiency that impels us to seek the indwelling power of God. Once we have known this ever-present help, we are equal to any situation. We can accept, without fear or resentment, the actions of others. This is not resignation but understanding. If the heart is filled with light, it cannot be darkened by self-pity. If the mind is established in principle, it cannot be disturbed by the conflicts which arise on the level of personality.

St. Paul spoke as one who had received the spirit of grace. A blessed presence came to him and possessed him, and he acknowledged himself the servant of that spirit. The apostle realized that the experience of the immediate fact of divine love was the beginning of a new life in truth. All that had gone before was changed in an instant. Paul admonished those who sincerely desire to grow and unfold to avail themselves of peace in Christ. Instead of waiting until pain of the soul or body frees us from the illusion of materiality, we should dedicate our internal capacities and abilities to spiritual growth. Once right motive inspires and directs our endeavors, we find that it is a gentle and kindly guidance. We are naturally happy because we are children of light, not darkness. We were fashioned with a wonderful capacity for quiet joy and serenity. We have been endowed with all that is necessary to live wisely and generously. We claim our birthright by a resolution of consciousness, and by this determination we find heaven even while we live upon the earth.

Long familiarity with the story of the Nazarene has bestowed an attitude of sincere regard for the nobility of his character and the integrity of his teachings. We are not in the presence of doctrines strange and distant to which we must convert ourselves with the energies of the mind or the intensities of our emotions. All that is necessary is to be still and allow consciousness itself to reveal its allegiances. We do not doubt the sublimity of the Christian mystery as it was originally revealed, but we must transform a passive admiration into an active participation. It is not enough that we possess the doctrine; the doctrine must possess us and direct our instincts and impulses.

Once we know that we live from Christ, we receive the strength which is not of this world. Those who keep the teachings of the Master are his disciples and have their share in him. There can be no consolation in faith until we share in its substance, and this sharing is the baptism of the spirit. In Western mysticism, a Christian is one who has received Christ in a mystery. There are many names given to the divine love which sustains those who have dedicated themselves to the way of heaven. But named or nameless, love perfects all the outer works of man, illumining them and giving them an authority which comes from the spirit.

We reach out with the longings of our souls toward the source of good. In those moments when we are inspired to kindly and thoughtful actions, we feel a growth of spirit within us. We wish that we could always abide in the peace of good works. Alas, we are no stronger than our faith, and we must experience through faith the inevitable victory of truth before our courage is sufficient to our needs. In order that this victory of reality may be accomplished in the mortal world, the way of salvation has been hidden within us. When the hour comes — and in every life it does come — when we must dedicate ourselves to the works of our Creator, we shall understand by a mystical apperception the words of St. Paul: "Christ in you, the hope of glory."

INDEX

Consciousness Studies Program

During 1997 PRS gathered together the latest research and data in the field of Consciousness Studies, with the purpose of developing a cutting-edge curriculum. PRS acquired a world class faculty to present these findings in a new non-residential program.

The individual one hour classes will be primarily on audio tape and some on video tape. The teachers will be accessible to the students by both E-mail and audio-conferencing. For more information call 323 663 2167 and ask for the Consciousness Studies program.

Fall

THE RELIGIOUS FUNCTION OF THE PSYCHE *Lionel Corbett* M.D.

CONSCIOUSNESS & CREATIVE COMMUNICATION
David E. Bresler Ph.D.

SCIENCE & SPIRITUALITY
Amit Goswami Ph.D.

WORLD RELIGIONS
Robert Ellwood Ph.D.

SPIRITUAL PHILOSOPHIES OF THE WEST *Stephan Hoeller* Ph.D.

Winter

SPIRITUAL PSYCHOLOGY
Robert Frager Ph.D.

PSY RESEARCH
Jeffrey Mishlove Ph.D.

SPIRITUAL UNIVERSE: QUANTUM PHYSICS & EXISTENCE OF THE SOUL
Fred Alan Wolf Ph.D.

MYSTERIES OF THE KABBALAH
Daniel C. Matt Ph.D.

UNDERSTANDING THE BIBLE
Culver Nelson D.D.

Spring

SELF REGULATION: THE FOUNDATION OF HUMAN POTENTIAL
Judith A. Green Ph.D. & *Robert Shellenberger* Ph.D.

UPANISHADS & BHAGAVAD GITA
Debashish Bannerji MSc.

BUDDHISM IN THE MODERN WORLD
B. Alan Wallace Ph.D.

OUTER & INNER CREATIVITY
Janelle B. Barlow Ph.D.

GNOSTICISM & THE PATH OF INNER KNOWLEDGE
Stephan Hoeller Ph.D.

Summer

PHYSICS OF THE SOUL
Amit Goswami Ph.D.

BODY HEALING & THE IMPLICATIONS
Martin L. Rossman M.D.

CLASSICAL PHILOSOPHY
Pierre Grimes Ph.D.

INTUITION IN BUSINESS
Marcia Emery Ph.D.

COSMOLOGY
Harold Dean Brown Ph.D.

Home Study Courses

Learning to Live By Living to Learn Course

COURSE DESCRIPTION: This unique home study course, one of a number of courses created by PRS founder Manly P. Hall, explores the four natures of the human body: the physical, the vital, the emotional, and the mental.

COURSE OBJECTIVES: The course is aimed at helping you gain an in-depth understanding of the four natures of the human being and the human body. All four aspects must work in harmony to enrich the inner life. Through this course, you can learn to build a personal life of value—to yourself and to society.

WHO CAN USE THIS COURSE?: This holistic approach to knowledge is suitable to persons of all ages, in all walks of life. There is no educational or other prerequisite other than your desire to learn.

CURRICULUM & COURSE MATERIALS: The course is divided into four units, each corresponding to the four natures. Each unit consists of ten lessons. All the course materials are derived from the vast invent᷿ Manly P. Hall's writings, including his lecture notes, PRS Journal articles spanning seventy years, and other writings.

FEES: For fees call PRS, Education Department, 3910 Los Feliz Blvd., Los Angeles, CA 90027, (323) 663-2167.

The Basic Ideas of Man Course

Manly P. Hall's life was devoted to researching, writing and lecturing on the basic and essential ideas which constitute the world's heritage of learning. It was his view that the real purpose of knowledge was to strengthen character, enrich living, and solve problems. As never before, such thinking is necessary.

His most cherished project was to establish a school of idealistic philosophy, by which the inherited wisdom of the ages could be made available in an orderly and sequential pattern. Only by such an interaction can the sincere student advance his or her knowledge and unfold his understanding naturally and effectively. For fees call the education department at (323) 663 2167. The only textbook required for the course is *Lectures on Ancient Philosophy.*